BEAUTIFUL PEOPLE

BEAUTIFUL PEOPLE

MAUREEN SEATON

&

AARON SMITH

BRIDWELL PRESS
Southern Methodist University
Dallas, Texas

Bridwell Press is the professional publishing arm of Bridwell Library
(SMU Libraries and Perkins School of Theology).
Southern Methodist University

SMU Libraries SMU Perkins School of Theology

Design by Alicia Beebe

Printed in the United States of America

ISBN: 978-1-957946-21-4 (hardback)
ISBN: 978-1-957946-22-1 (paperback)
ISBN: 978-1-957946-26-9 (epub)

Cover image: *Girls with Dinosaur* by Joshua Benmore

for Denise Duhamel

&

for James Allen Hall

Contents

Introduction

Maureen Seaton and I became friends through writing this book. I'd been a fan of her work since graduate school when I discovered her book *Furious Cooking*, which won the 1995 Iowa Poetry Prize. (I still carry that book with me when I travel.) Though Maureen and I had not spent time together, we were connected via friends and poetry. There seemed to be a sense in the early 2000s, too, that queer writers knew each other, perhaps more than we did. In addition to meeting at a conference, she wrote to me once about some poems she wanted to submit to the queer literary magazine *Bloom* when I was its poetry editor. I can't imagine I did not profess my love of her work during that exchange.

In the fall of 2021, I decided to teach *Furious Cooking* to my undergraduates. In my fifteen years of teaching, I'd never taught the book because "the rule" that had been hammered into my brain was that one should never teach a book they love; I'm glad I ignored that advice. Not only did I teach the book, but I invited Maureen to class. I knew that Maureen had metastatic breast cancer, but a friend told me she was still somewhat active. It was during Covid when everyone was using Zoom, which was maybe the only good thing to come from the pandemic: we figured out how to have literary community and to connect in ways we never had before. Maureen said yes.

The students loved the book, and they loved Maureen. She was generous, smart, down-to-earth, and funny. Her chihuahua, Binky, barked through a few portions of the class. (The students and I found it entertaining.) Later, Maureen and I would bond over our chihuahuas. We even spoke on the phone after I had to put mine (Alice Neel) to sleep. She wanted to know the whole story. When I told her the process was peaceful, gentle, and profoundly important, she thanked me and said that hearing the story made her realize she wanted that kind of death for herself.

Shortly after the class, Maureen wrote to me and said she'd a felt a connection between us during the class and wanted to be in touch more. I told her I felt the same. It didn't take long before we arrived at collaborating. I knew Maureen collaborated often with Denise Duhamel (flip this book over to read their book *Tilt*); their book *Exquisite Politics* was the first collaborative book I'd read. I also knew that she and Denise, along with our friend the poet David Trinidad, had edited *Saints of Hysteria: A Half-Century of Collaborative American Poetry*. That was all I knew about collaborative poetry. I wasn't sure what the process would be like. I wasn't sure if the project would go anywhere.

Here's a secret: I never wanted to collaborate. I always thought the poems wouldn't feel like mine and that I would put a great deal of effort into something that ultimately wouldn't interest me. My sister is a songwriter, and her world is all about collaborating; she told me once that more than one person in a writing session pushes a song to a place that it would never go if someone tried to create it alone. I don't know why I didn't have faith in the process for poetry. Perhaps it's because my own work often mines autobiography, and I thought that had something to do with solitude. I would soon find that it didn't.

The collaboration happened over email. Our process was straightforward: we would pick a title and write several sections, alternating back and forth, riffing on the subject. "Beautiful People" was our first section, and then we continued with different "types" of people. I began the pieces, and Maureen decided when they ended. We wrote as much as we wanted in our sections, in any style we wanted, and when we finished, we gave each other the first line the other had to use to start their new section. The writing throughout the book is labeled with our initials. There are two sestinas at the end of the book, and we wrote those alternating back and forth with each line. That is also true for two of the sonnets in the crown of sonnets in the section "Queer People."

What I found happening during the process (and what Maureen knew would happen) was that a door of permission opened. Every time it was my turn, I pushed myself in different directions, hoping to write something that would excite Maureen and make her want to write. I surprised myself. I think Maureen felt the same. Collaboration inspired me to take chances I never would have in my own poems; it widened the lens that I looked through and allowed me to see in different ways. It also allowed me to write in a different voice. Maureen explained it best on my podcast *Breaking Form* that I host with the poet James Allen Hall. (In fact, if you listen to episode 53, "Just Keep Going," you can hear us discuss the process.) Maureen said that because we went back and forth and wrote as much as we wanted in our sections, she felt that four voices emerged. My voice is the first, hers is the second, and then the *other* Aaron is the third, which makes the *other* Maureen the fourth voice.

Maureen's mastery and love of traditional forms made me want to experiment. I wrote my first successful sestina ("Leading Men") and also one of my favorite sonnets ("Sissy"), which was featured on the Academy of American Poets' *Poem-a-Day*. The title poem of Maureen's final book, *The Sky Is an Elephant*, was written during our collaboration. She was also in love with the rondelet and wrote some for this book, including "Rondelet for the Terminally Ill," which also appears in her final book. Her esteem for the rondelet made me want to try a triolet.

Imagine geeking out about your favorite subject with one of your favorite people; this is what the process was like. I think Maureen would agree that had we not been in conversation, these poems would not exist. I think she would also agree that we not only made a book, but we also made a friendship. When Maureen was dying, her daughter Emily wrote to me and asked me to send the most recent version of the book because Maureen wanted Emily to read it to her. Even if this book had never been published, the fact that she wanted our words with her at the end would be enough.

Maureen and I did one Zoom call to edit the book, and then our relationship became less about writing and more about our friendship, cemented via emails and texts. We wrote a few more things, but what ultimately became *Beautiful People* was completed during the winter, spring, and summer months of 2022. Because we only got to edit the book once, it still needed more cohesion. After some distance, and with the help of our wonderful editor, I was able to see where some parts of the book, while interesting, were not quite pulling their weight. I was concerned about editing the book further after Maureen's death. I reached out to Denise to get her advice. Denise wrote back that Maureen was "the QUEEN of cutting/revising so whatever you do will be fine with her—I just know it."

Keeping Denise's words in mind, I worked my way through the manuscript. My guiding principle was to highlight the places where the writing was the most engaging, daring, or surprising, while maintaining the integrity of the exchange, of the energy that kept us going for so many months. I tried not to change any words that Maureen wrote (and only changed a very few of mine) unless a larger edit made something unclear. I wanted the book to be what we wrote when we wrote it, even if I had to cut some parts to keep the integrity of our process. I'm happy to have the sections that did not make it into this book still saved on my computer; they have more personal significance than literary value, and I cherish them as a document of our friendship. Ultimately, they set the stage for us to find the center of the pieces—the work that, I hope, rises to artistry.

Sometimes, when I'm driving and see a particularly beautiful sky or a string of birds perched on a telephone wire, I think: *I bet Maureen would like that.* Reading through this book today, I feel the same thing. I hope you, reader, like it, too.

Aaron Smith, Nashville, TN
August 2025

Beautiful People

A

The male supermodel on Instagram tells me about mental health and how he can't be sad when he sees palm trees and I can barely look at his face or listen because he's shirtless and his nipples are just off camera and I'm looking for a hint of them. Because I'm average and unhappy and don't take trips to palm trees and walk around in my underwear for money, it doesn't make me feel better to know beautiful people struggle, too. I hate beautiful people

M

who drive VW buses to Woodstock instead of me because I'm slipping off a barstool, but I digress. It was so funny, no, scary, when my lover came to visit with her new iPhone slash freaking amazing camera and took off around my Crest-white neighborhood photographing fall flora with glee and abandon and I said be careful, honey, and she threw me some kind of shade and walked right up to Mr. Pale's house and snapped a shot of his quaking aspens. Lovers:

A

a friend of a friend fell in love at a Madonna (Cher) concert, got fake-married, flipped their car on Interstate 65 near Dinosaur World in Kentucky, and died. Remember when we sat in traffic 800 summers ago because there was an accident and you told me not to run the air conditioner because we needed to save gas, and I told you I had hot crotch and was sticking to the seat? I still wonder whose wreck we were sitting behind. Whose heartache we were at the beginning of.

Dear Dead Gay Boys
Dear Erased Pterodactyls
Dear Family of Five Killed Side by Side Munching Chemical-Stuffed Twinkies and Doritos
Dear Dead Baby Sick of Car Seat and Heat
Dear Our Past Selves Speeding Eyes Shut through the Years.

What I'm trying

M

to say is that I can't imagine skiing. Not after crashing into an entire crowd of bystanders when I was twelve and went with my class to a mountain in upstate New York and came down the bunny slope at 30 miles an hour without first having learned how to stop. Living in Colorado now is not funny. Skiers and wildfires. The other day there was a fire in Boulder and we thought we were going to have to evacuate. Three dogs, a grouchy eight-year-old, my daughter with a broken leg, my sleepy son-in-law, and me, on chemo. Still my lover is coming to visit soon. She will bring her camera again and this time take pictures of spring flowers up close. It's her new thing and it turns me on. Columbine, fireweed, elephant head lousewort. (See Robert Hass, "The Garden of Delight.")

A

I'm trying to practice more love these days and live with intention.
I even say the word *manifest* without laughing. I repeat: *money is running*

through the streets to find me. Last week, I found two quarters on the sidewalk
outside Old Navy. Hey, people have built whole religions on things less

tangible. Sometimes, depending on the day, I believe in luck. In the early
2000s, I'd get excited to see a 212 number (old New York) on my phone,

like maybe it was a call that would change my life forever. It never did. It was
usually Con Ed asking about my bill, or the occasional telemarketer. Whether

we admit it or not, everyone would like for fate to pick them out of a crowd,
for something extraordinary, something completely unearned to happen.

M

Corpus Hypercubus (Salvador Dalí, 1954)

Pardon me, are you Jesus?
Your cross is a tesseract.
Did you know that when you agreed to die?
Is that Mary Magdalene gazing up at you or Dalí's wife, Gala?

Is a tesseract the best way to time travel?
Do you know Thor? Of course you do. What about Robert Downey, Jr.?
Are you familiar with the phrase, *Beam me up*?

Your body could be a swimmer's body. You could be a dancer or a model.
Still, something's holding you in mid-air.
String theory? Grace?

Tesseracts have eight cubes and yours look like wood. Did you build them yourself?
Are you surreal or are you a philosophical interpretation of quantum mechanics?
Is Gala/Mary hoping for a chess game? Queen's Gambit, anyone?

So I wrote this poem while my body was unwittingly engaged in the physics of dying. Meaning, all of a sudden I was not so much body as something (okay, soul) that could slip in and out of consciousness at will (although not *my* will, evidently) and experience "somewhere else." (Notice I do not say exactly where "somewhere else" might be because I still have no idea other than that I was there. Hmmm.) Thank you for listening. (I am making this

A

up.) Up, and away!

Corpus Hypercubus Flipped (Salvador Dalí, 1954-ish)

Is Gala/Mary hoping
for a chess game? Queen's
Gambit, anyone? Are you surreal

or are you a philosophical interpretation
of quantum mechanics? Tesseracts
have eight cubes and yours

look like wood. Did you build them
yourself? String theory? Grace? Still,
something's holding you in mid-air.

Your body could be a swimmer's
body. You could be a dancer
or a model. Are you familiar with

the phrase, *Beam me up*? Do you know
Thor? Of course you do. What about
Robert Downey, Jr.? Is a tesseract

the best way to time travel? Is that
Mary Magdalene gazing up at you
or Dalí's wife, Gala? Your cross

is a tesseract. Did you know
that when you agreed to die?
Pardon me, are you Jesus?

Lucky People

A

I read somewhere that you'd have to fly every day for 18,000 years to
even have a 50% chance of crashing, yet I'd still rather drive. There's

science to explain why when you're thinking about someone they call,
but isn't science itself the miracle? According to the National Endowment

for Financial Education, 70% of people who win the lottery end up
broke and a third go on to declare bankruptcy, but a New York man

won the lottery twice: $10 million in 2019 and $10 million, again, in 2022.
I've never won more than two dollars from a scratch off, but I love

using the losing tickets to clean my teeth. It makes me so damn happy!
The man took his winnings in two lump sums of $6,510,000, which is

$13,020,000. God! What a beautiful number! I guess what I'm trying

M

to say is, Congratulations! You've won another day!

Death-in-Paradise Rondelet w/Shorebirds

I'm thrilled to be
Still alive in Paradise or
I'm thrilled to be
Salty, human, off spying on
Cormorants in their morning suits
Pelicans in boots. Ah, lucky
Me: thrilled to be!

(A rondelet for Aaron, who never imagined

A

he'd write a sestina.)

Leading Men

Thelma and Louise and a blow-dryer made Brad Pitt
a star. *The Notebook* made Ryan Gosling
a household name. *Casino Royale* is why Daniel Craig
is *Daniel Craig*. *London* was where I first saw Chris Evans,
but have you seen his chest in *Captain America?* Chris Hemsworth
(that chest!) got my attention in *Thor.* Colin Farrell

is the best in *Fright Night*. I love Colin Farrell
the most, though, in *Seven Psychopaths*. He and Brad Pitt
should make a movie together. Chris Hemsworth
and Ryan Gosling should, too. (Don't confuse Ryan Gosling
with Ryan Reynolds.) It's hard to believe Chris Evans
did an ensemble piece—*Knives Out*—with Daniel Craig.

Captain America and James Bond in the same movie! Daniel Craig
is a terrific actor—stage *and* screen—but when Colin Farrell
cries in *In Bruges*, he's hard to beat. Chris Evans
is handsome, but he's not a "great" actor. Brad Pitt
is good, but he probably got the Oscar for being shirtless. Ryan Gosling
is great, too. He's more serious than Chris Hemsworth,

but do we really care if he's serious? Chris Hemsworth's
glowing torso is almost as magical as Daniel Craig
emerging from the ocean in a blue Speedo. Ryan Gosling's
abs in *Crazy, Stupid, Love* are crazy, stupid, and loved. Colin Farrell—
if you like lean and cut—is right up there with Brad Pitt.
Okay, Brad Pitt's body is better. Chris Evans

is the most "jock" hot *and* Chris Evans
has a great cock (accidentally leaked online). Chris Hemsworth's
dick isn't online, but I've seen Brad Pitt's
in *Playgirl* (yum), and Daniel Craig's
floats in the bathtub in *Love Is the Devil* (slurp). Colin Farrell
shows his thick dick in a sex tape. (*Watch* it!) Ryan Gosling's

cock is online, too. Someone snapped him peeing. Ryan Gosling
cries well in *Lars and the Real Girl*. Chris Evans?
His pecs make me weep. Again, Colin Farrell,
in *In Bruges*, is one of my all-time fave cries. Chris Hemsworth
doesn't cry, or maybe he does? Again, does it matter? (Those arms!) Daniel Craig
does a great almost-cry in *Flashbacks of a Fool* (bad movie). Brad Pitt

cries a lot. In *Fight Club* he's as hot as Chris Evans, Chris Hemsworth,
Colin Farrell, and Ryan Gosling combined. Between Daniel Craig
and Brad Pitt? I can't believe I'm saying this: Brad Pitt.

Sad People

A

To Whom It May Concern:

I wanted to call this poem "Funny People" or "Smart People" or "Queer People,"
but I decided on "Sad People" because I'm sad today and can't help it.

I've tried: Lexapro
Effexor
Paxil
Pristiq
Lamotrigine
Celexa
Modafinil
Lunesta
Clonazepam

My mom's dead and today is my parents' anniversary, but I don't think that's why I'm sad. I'm always a little sad. The main character in *The Lover* by Marguerite Duras says she's always a little sad. I read that Duras said that book was silly and that she wrote it drunk in an airport. I wrote my last two books on weed, and the third one, *Primer,* I revised while high.

A student told me they couldn't read about self-harm and spelled it: s#lf h#rm, as if erasing the word could erase the _________. If that were the case, dear friend, I could write *I'm happy, I'm happy, I'm happy*. Of course, this poem is for you, Maureen, but I only wanted you to be concerned

M

if you wanted to be a poet (let's pretend we're not) (yet), like who would you be? (Besides yourself or me, of course.) I just read some essays online about Spicer and Lorca and magic and duende and my friend L. is taking a class on tarot which I gave up for a long time because I constantly got mean cards and L. felt sorry for me so I finally stopped taroting and then picked it up again when I found goddess cards instead of tarot.

The Sky Is an Elephant

Once I was the little girl who invented the universe.
I was sad as a chimney without a house.
I didn't mean this to be a poem, but it's building itself
and there is nothing I can do to stop it, truly, try
and stop me. I am sad as a house without a doll. See?
A doll without a mouth. A mouth without a smile. (Note
to poet: revise that last part, it's boring.) Here's a line
from Spicer or Lorca—who cares? (They don't.)
But the sky is an elephant / and the jasmines are water without blood.
This is sad but it makes me happy, especially the elephant.
I think this poem actually ended somewhere around
the doll or the mouth, but I am too sad to fix it,
you know how that feels. So this makebelieve poem
will go on as is, like the moon over the skeleton of a girl.

(a translation for Aaron Smith, my idol, with love).

Happy People

A

I get sad
that I have
to work
to be happy,
but I decided
to be nicer
to myself
and my
complicated
brain. I think
of R.E.M.
and being
shiny does
make me
happy. This week
I bought
a shirt with
FANCY
FUCKER
written in sequins
across the front.

I don't
necessarily feel
fancy, but I do
like thinking
of myself
as a happy
fucker. Maybe
my happiness
just has an
edge? Maybe
the edge
is my
happiness?

M

The thing about happiness is that it is both shiny & yummy. Glittery & delicious. Bright colors & whipped cream. Libras are supposed to be materialistic, which I'm not at all, which, I think, is because almost all of my planets are in Scorpio, a wizened, magic, sex-happy sign that doesn't even know if she's got her clothes on much less if they glow. Talk about an edge!

A

I'm happy that I don't have a car payment
or a student loan payment
(I won't mention the credit cards. Ha!).
I'm happy about parentheticals
and exclamation points and songs online
that are free, donuts and tacos and how I love/
hate Doritos. I am happy about
colors, deep,
deep blues,
serious greens,

M

fiery pinks,
disastrous purples,
rebellious reds…

I was so happy when I realized that the one thing I'm certain will still be there when I kick the bucket is music. Music and color. What more does a soul need? I have a dancey soul with a sick Irish sense of humor like my grandmother, who once dressed up as a burglar on Halloween, barged into our house, and stole all our candy. Only the dog knew it was her. He didn't bat an eye.

crazy people,
smart dogs,
Skittles,
candy corn,
M&M's,

A

Reese's Pieces
make me think

of Drew Barrymore
who was in *E.T.*

and who doesn't
need a talk show,

though she has one,
and I can't believe

Cameron Diaz (Drew's
friend) retired,

I guess I can
believe it, but I miss

her in movies.
She is so good

in *In Her Shoes*
when she reads

out loud Eliz-
abeth Bishop's

"One Art."

I won't drag us down a sonnet hole (*Write* it!) like in our forthcoming "Queer People," but here is a "sissy" sonnet for you:

Sissy

I can't remember my dad calling me a sissy,
but he definitely told me not to be a sissy.
I secretly (or not so secretly) liked all the sissy
things. We had a hunting dog named Sissy.
Really: Sissy. My father nicknamed my sister: Sissy.
Still, he says, "How's Sissy?" and calls her Sissy
when she goes home to visit him. Belinda (Sissy)
is one of the toughest people I know. My sissy
(sister) has kicked someone's ass, which isn't sissy-
ish, I guess, though I want to redefine sissy
into something fabulous, tough, tender, "sissy-
tough." Drag queens are damn tough and sissies.
I'm pretty fucking tough and a big, big sissy,
too. And kind. Tough and kind and happy: a sissy.

M

Your sissy sonnet made me cry. It's very cool. And fun as hell as well. You are my favorite living sonneteer! Your last line is simply gorgeous!

Here is one for you:

Colorado

Spirits of newly dead sunflowers
and a red lighthouse above a well-fed
bookcase. Is it true I once loved Springsteen?
I drive haphazardly, arriving nowhere.
Maybe somewhere, sometimes. Dark birds impaled
on hawthorn trees, women fibrillating
in the altitude. What spills beneath the door
that started at the sea and flooded westward,
congealing in a breast with salt and blood
and imagining who lives in the rest
of this unsettled house? This is where grief
meets more than silence, the shepherd next door
barking psychotically, cars on Baseline
swishing past. Coyotes on the open lands

suspended in the supermoonlight.

Lost People

M

There's no one more lost
than the big shot so lost
he doesn't know he's lost.
There's no one more lost
at sea, no one more lost
at sky, no one more lost
than he who kissed his lost
heart goodbye.

Dear Clockmaker

after Remedios Varo, *Revelation or the Clockmaker*, 1955

You think you know all there is to know
about the direction of time, so it's no
mystery that all your grandfathers stand
poised to chime at three, a synchronicity
deserving of recognition or precog-
nition or, in this case, apparition,
for here comes a sliver of time twirling
through your window (to your revelation
and awe), and suddenly your beloved
clockparts go crashing to the floor (a horo-
logical sleight of hand) and that whirling
disc seems a lot more Einsteinian than New-
tonian, and you thought you knew all along
what there was to know about the mystery
of the direction of time. But you were wrong.

Mystical People

A

My Enneagram number is 4, and tonight, by accident, I discovered Nuclear Mysticism, the philosophical interpretation of quantum mechanics. Aren't we always trying to explain the mess of consciousness, the actual vs. the perceived?

M

My grandson just walked by with a huge yellow play gun that shoots plastic darts. I think his Enneagram is a 6. I think he may be a priest someday. By then I will most certainly be dead and ecstatically surrounded by dogs, which I was grateful to learn in my first Nuclear Mysticism class taught by an old hippie at the top of Longs Peak which you can see from our house.

A

After my mother died, I walked around in a sort of airtight shell, or in my brain there was a door I could only approach before it vanished. I thought I was open and dealing with her death, but then I stopped listening to music (Sufjan Stevens's *Carrie & Lowell* could put me in bed).

M

Rondelet for the Terminally Ill

To understand a thing is a bridge...—Carl Jung

Stand on a bridge
There, in the center, facing North.
Feel the whole bridge
Collapse beneath you: Goodbye, bridge.
North, South, East, West, Above, Below.
Hold still and feel the directions.
Now be the bridge.

Back to

A

physics, or a triolet for the scientifically challenged

physics is hard-
er than the hard-
est calculus and
physics is hard-
er than the hardest cand-
y. understand?
physics is hard-
er than hard.

Three Jokes about Atoms:

1) Wanna know why you can't trust an atom? They make up literally everything.
2) The proton is not speaking to the other proton. He's mad atom.
3) What did one charged atom say to the other? I got my ion you!

The last time I laughed

M

really hard was this morning on the phone with my friend Sally, who came through cancer
decades ago and is great for laughing. We laughed for an hour about the pandemic

and depression and extroverts and then she had to go solve some physics problems left over
from the people in her life who have transitioned to philosophy. Suffice it to say that P=MS2.

Philosophically speaking, I don't belong on the science track now any more than I did
all those years ago when I was fainting in Chemistry—low blood pressure, low blood,

who stole my blood? I also fainted in Calculus, sometimes in Gym, oh, I love your triolet!

A

When you wrote "fainting in Chemistry," I read "fainting in Christianity," and *that* is something I *can* talk about. I got baptized in Mill Creek when I was ten.

My grandfather on one side and the pervy assistant preacher on the other. They dunked me under while people sang hymns on the shore. There was a man on a boat—

not part of our church—fishing behind me. *God will make you fishers of men* (something like that). The perv wore white sport socks with plaid pants and once said that God

told him to watch porn for "informational purposes." I'm not sure what else to say about that. What *can* be said about that? I watch porn to get off. I'm tired

M

of sex. I sure am! So much depends upon red panties glazed with Astroglide beside the white fox fur. Am I right? I am too through. I am suddenly wanting to have sex with a doctor!

I almost said I fainted in church before—you read my mind! Turns out I was hypoglycemic and no one knew and since I was alive (if young) when Catholics had to fast from midnight to go to

Communion (eat Jesus) (there I go with sex again) and my family always went to late Mass, I often fainted before I had a chance to stick my tongue out. I avoided the subject in that stuff I

wrote to you because I really liked communion and was horribly disappointed to be dragged out of church before I could have it and I didn't want to admit that. I was a big Jesus fan all the way up to

the day I excommunicated myself for having sex with a priest. Maybe I would have liked physics more if you were my teacher. As it turns out, I ended up reading my daughter's physics book after

we moved to Chicago and I suddenly got the whole picture. Life fell into place like a tired old sex scandal and I was glazed all over with rainwater.

Straight People

A: Sometimes straight people eat Neapolitan ice cream and sometimes they make laws to make gay people feel bad about themselves.

M: Sometimes straight people think that being gay is just too much. Too much fun, that is!

A: Sometimes straight people build big white houses in big white neighborhoods and drive white SUVs that they park in multi-car garages. They have parties on weekends and sit on their big back porches in white T-shirts and white hats and use white napkins and white paper plates. Sometimes these straight people have babies, too, and send them to private schools.

M: Sometimes straight people aren't really that straight and therein lies quite the problem for some straight people, not to mention gay people, of course, who don't really know (for sure) which straight people are actually straight and which straight people are actually gay. It is often the case that even the straightest of people can be gay underneath, so I (who am completely gay most of the time) think it's a good idea for gay folks to watch out for straight ones, especially if they hate us.

A: Sometimes straight people are kind of dumb, and I think it would be funny if we stopped talking about them and instead started talking about funny people:

Funny People

A

Joke Pantoum

Knock, knock. Knock, knock.
Who's there? Who's there?
Knock, knock. Knock, knock.
Who's there? Who's there?

Who's there? Who's there?
Funny poets. Funny poets.
Who's there? Who's there?
Funny poems by funny poets.

Funny poets. Funny poets.
Funny poets: Who? Who?
Funny poets. Funny poets.
Funny poets: Who? Who?

Funny poets: Who? Who?
Funny poets Maureen and Aaron.
Funny poems by funny poets.
Funny poets Maureen and Aaron.

Queer People

A

During the pandemic I started collecting Ken
dolls. One so hot I worried I was attracted to
him: long blond hair, slick plastic body, nipples I drew
on with a brown Sharpie. I wondered what it would say
about me if I started taking Ken on dates and
fucking him? But would it have really hurt anyone?
I bought him slutty shorts off eBay and stood him on
the shelf by the most fabulous Barbie! Long black hair,
rainbow dress. (I didn't want him to be lonely when
I was working.) I wanted to make the faggiest
Christmas scene you'd ever seen: rainbow lights, glittery
ornaments, dolls in Santa hats and fab outfits. It
was miraculous! Jesus wasn't the reason, but,
darling, he would have died for the fabulosity.

M

You know what else is fabulous? I prefer Ken
to Barbie too! Fabulous? Or fabulated? Who knows?
(To engage in the composition of fables, especially
those featuring a strong element of fantasy.) Okay,
here's the scoop for anyone who cares to know
who I loved as a kid or who I now love or who
I will ever love: Olive Oyl. Soft and stringy,
screechy and bendable, my buddy, my pal, my
charismatic pre-feminist-theory lover of good old
Popeye the Sailor Man. (Barbie is simply too smooth.)
The first thing my son said when he opened this Ken doll was,
"He has real leather pants!" He definitely likes the way
this Ken doll (he named him Aaron) looks and is a big fan
of his fancy clothes and super cool hair. (Johns Creek, GA, US)

A

Earring Magic Ken has his own Wikipedia page
and apparently gay men bought the doll in *droves*.
What wasn't to love? Blond highlights, lavender
mesh shirt, purple leather vest, earring in his left
ear, and the circular charm on his necklace that
everyone thought was a cock ring. Because of that
Mattel discontinued the doll and recalled him from
stores. But Ken didn't have a cock, so he certainly
didn't need to put a ring on it (cue Beyoncé). Which
makes me think how gay men love divas: Whitney,
Britney, Cher, Mariah, Gaga, Madonna, Judy, Barbra,
Liza, Donna, Diana, Dolly, Bette, Janet, Kylie, RuPaul,
J.Hud, Dusty, Celine, Wonder Woman, and Bey (obvi).
The Billy doll needed the cock ring. I wish I could sing.

M

When I'm sad, I sing in the car. When I'm happy,
I sing (and dance) in my bedroom and hope
no one hears me (or, for that matter, sees me). My
divas are Patti, Laura, Joni, Stevie, Sting, & Santana.
That is my (extremely) short list, but my actual list
is crazy long, so I will send you that by sestina soon.
I know gay men's divas are sacred in a slightly different
way than mine, as I'm kind of a Mary Magdalene freak.
Mary's Wikipedia page says she had seven demons driven
right out of her and I've had at least that many driven
out of me or into me, depending. Much of my life
has been spent restoring the demons that were batted
out of the park along the way. For example: happiness,
raucous laughter, lawless sonnets, & of course, sex.

A

Lately, there's nothing I crave more than an unexpected donut or scone. Yep, some homosexuals like carbs. I'd say most queers do, even if they don't let themselves eat them. I live in a converted church which makes sense because I *am* a converted church. Anyway, I spent my first year living there collecting icons, mostly from the Catholic store in Pittsburgh. The nuns get them from old churches. They say they are blessed or sanctified or whatever holy-moly priests do when they're not making you feel bad about your body and birth control. V Mary, Francis the Sissy, Catherine, Sebastian, and the one whose name I can't remember standing on Satan with a spear. I'm not Catholic, but I have so many I had to stop buying them because the man I was sleeping with thought I was crazy. (St. Michael!) I am!

M

Crazy, isn't it? How somewhere, right now, another queer
is not having sex? And neither is yet another queer
even thinking of having sex or thinking of sex queerly.
Queers might all be sleeping (queerfully) now, it's as queer
and simple as that. Or take that VW of whiskery queers
heading out for their camping trip (often, not always, queers
with baseball caps and/or bear whistles), from queerish
places like Nashville or Boulder, to places where queers
gather outdoors and make campfires perfectly queerly,
(with sparklers and James Beard), and also yummy Queer
Burgers (with blue cheese stuffing) and our famous Queer
Furters (pigs in doughy blankets). How gluten-queer
is that? And before I get all queerified and queerful
let me state: Sex is the bomb, oh yeah, when you're queer!

A

The first time I came across a bunch of rowdy lesbians was at an outdoor wedding in Columbus, Ohio. It was long before marriage really *counted*, but those dykes didn't care. They were buckeye dykes, swing-state dykes, rowdy dykes, not dykes on bikes, but I'm sure they had some (and guns, too!). There were guys in skirts with purses, but it was all about the volleyball and sports bras and when coolers needed moved (full of queer beers, dykey Cokes, lezzy sodas, and gay-ass waters) the women carried them. Nobody asked the men or needed them. Of course, I know now women can do anything (duh!), but I was young and from West Virginia where men did the heavy shit and women didn't lift. There was no prince that day, or fairytale bullshit, just women in love and thirsty guests grabbing drinks from coolers.

M

My favorite queer story begins with a lie and ends with one
old song by Michael Nesmith of the Monkees called
"Different Drum," which is what I've often drummed to,
I mean sung to, although I've never heard Nesmith sing it,
only Linda Ronstadt and the Stone Poneys during my short
stint in college before my parents kicked me out for thinking
too much or drinking too much or marching too much or
having too much sex with the bartender. (The lie.)
Turns out that Nesmith's single mom, Bette, invented
Liquid Paper in her garage and sold it for $48 million.
Oh, don't get me wrong, it's not that I'm knockin' it,
It's just that I am not in the market (best off-rhyme ever)
For a boy who wants to love only me… (sorry, Bartender)
We'll both live a lot longer if you live without me.

A

That time someone tried to pull the reins in on me, I
followed them into an ATM vestibule and told them
to fuck off. That was before I was afraid of people and
stayed home all the time and only left the house between
10 and 2. But I don't want to be sad in this sonnet, if it's
really a sonnet and not a sort-of sonnet, but even sort-of
sonnets are sonnets now, right? Now for the joy: I went
to Red Robin for raspberry iced tea and endless fries and
dipped them in "extra ranch, please." I scrolled vacation
spots on my phone because life is short (cliché!) (true!) and
I should travel more. Did you know at the Blue Lagoon in
Iceland everyone has to shower completely naked before they
get into the water? I'm not sure why that made me happy, but
it did. Can you imagine being the person who enforces that?

M

My favorite people are queers and my favorite ice cream is
Naked Berry. (I made that flavor up, doesn't it sound cool?)
My favorite people really are queers. And poets. "Real"
sonnets are even more fun to make than "sort-of-sonnets" if you
like puzzles or counting or listening so hard your heart breaks.
That ten-syllable line will keep you prisoner, though.
Before you know it, you'll be up late talking to yourself
in pentameter. You might even forget anything exists
that isn't made of iambs, little creatures with their legs blown off
running from side to side before you on the page. Like:
It's very well to say, creation thrives (a line from Marilyn Hacker's
sonnet, "On Marriage"). Personally, I lose my beat in marriage
but I do like keeping it across a line, like this one (also by Hacker):
which means that we must choose, and choose, and choose.

A

Or Ginsberg in 1948: *Together into the Woe of the blazing bell—*
I find myself winded, thinking of Ginsberg's American, breath-filled lines tipping the page nearly over. God that line makes me nervous. I want to fix it,
but I won't go near it again or think about it. My friend
James kept pronouncing a name wrong and instead of correcting
him, I started saying it the same way he did. I didn't want
to hurt his feelings. I should work on that in therapy, but I've
worked on so many things I don't want to work anymore.
Meanwhile, I have a consultation with a surgeon for a neck
lift. Is it really what's on the inside that matters? *Aren't therapists*
the best, Diane said, *unless they're shitty*. What if I made this sonnet
thirteen lines instead of fourteen? Would it still be a sonnet?
If I counted syllables like in my first one, would it be better?
This poem isn't perfect, friend, but I promise it was written with love.

A&M

If I'm being honest, I'm worried about the long line, Maureen.
That long line is Ginsbergian! He loves it and so do I, Aaron.
That makes me happy, Maureen! I thought: I hope Maureen
Will someday soon meet Ginsberg and he'll tell her that I (Aaron)
Went clubbing when he died (my mom's B-day). He'll say, Maureen,
Don't worry about the goofy-spooky of it all. And, Aaron,
It's always the right time to dance, ask Kylie Minogue, ask Maureen
If she knows who Kylie Minogue is, or who that is in the mirror, Aaron.
Probably not Kylie, but I know the mirror woman is lovely, Maureen!
Mirror women cast a long glance at the reflected world, right, Aaron?
Right, Maureen! And if you listen closely they speak: *Dear Maureen,*
Do not fret that you are becoming more invisible by the day. Ask Aaron:
Is vanishing just another way that we arrive at love? Aaron, Maureen,
You've made it through twelve sonnets together. Maureen & Aaron,

A

just three more to go for a Heroic Crown. How else will we ever know what it feels like to be:::
:::::::::::::::::::::::::::::::::::::Freddie Mercury in a crown and red cape (1986)
:::::::::::::::::::::Elton John in a crown in a Super Bowl commercial (2012)
::::::::::::::::::::::::::Rihanna in a crown looking sort of like the Pope (2018)
::Lil Nas X in a crown in the *Guardian* (2020)
::Kristen Stewart in a crown in *Spencer* (2021)
::::::::::Lady Gaga in a black crown and glasses in "Bad Romance" (2009)
:::::::::::::Madonna in crown and eye patch on the Madame X tour (2019)
::::::::::::::::::::::::::::::::::::Jay-Z rapping "Crown" on *Magna Carta*...(2013)
:::::::::::::::::::::Vanessa Williams in a crown before she posed nude (1983)
:::Cher in a crown in Zurich (2019)
:::::::::::::::::::::::::::::::::::Beyoncé in a crown on the Grammys (2017)
FreddieEltonRihannaLilNasXKristenGagaMadgeJay-ZVanessaCherBey

M

Listen up, queers of the world! There's something I've been meaning
to say and yet here I am not saying it, and not only am I not
saying the thing I've been meaning to say since, I don't know,
1st grade, but I am also deciding not to say it in a sonnet,
which is not a real sonnet because I've decided that no one can say
how to say it, even the first sonnet-maker whose name
eludes me or seduces me, either way, I am simply a person whose
fingers are moving fast, like really too fast, I'm pretty sure, since

I could use a break or break a finger, although notice I just
skipped a line? (Maybe the sonnet broke a stanza.) The thing I am
not saying (and I have 3 more lines not to say it), approaches from the left,
riding along my peripheral vision like a revelation that will thunder
noisily through my neighborhood and park in front of my house
in an old blue truck with the dilapidated giddy sign: *I Love You*.

A&M

Here's the scoop for anyone who cares to know:
Lately, there's nothing I crave more than an unexpected
charismatic pre-feminist-theory lover of good old
women in love and thirsty guests grabbing drinks from coolers.
Crazy, isn't it? How somewhere, right now, another queer
I was sleeping with thought I was crazy. (St. Michael!) I am!
When I'm sad, I sing in the car. When I'm happy,
I find myself winded, thinking of Ginsberg's American, breath-filled lines tipping the page nearly
saying the thing I've been meaning to say since, I don't know,
the first time I came across a bunch of rowdy lesbians
running from side to side before you on the page. Like:
before you know it, you'll be up late talking to yourself
in an old blue truck with the dilapidated giddy sign: *I Love You*.
My favorite queer story begins with a lie and ends with one.

Holy People

A

eat Big Macs after church on Sundays, or they go to places like Cracker Barrel and Outback and sit in their Sunday clothes with others sitting in *their* Sunday clothes knowing the wait might be 45 minutes or longer, but that's not long when they have eternity to look forward to with streets of gold and gigantic mansions.

That's my childhood religion, Maureen, bible-thumping, body-hating, shame-making, queer-erasing fundamentalists. I wonder

M

if growing up Catholic was any better?

If growing up Catholic was any better than fundamentalism I wouldn't have anything to write about right now, although when my Saturn returned—the first time, when I was 27—it knocked the Catholic right out of me and something else into me that I can only call happy. But we're writing about Holy People, not Happy People, so: Are holy people happy, do you think? I don't think so, really. If I were holy I would have to stop swearing, for one thing, and that would make me unhappy. I would have to not have sex with myself or anyone else I wasn't married to and, in my case, of course, who wasn't a man. That would be a cross to bear for sure. I am so sorry you grew up around all that shaming, Aaron. My childhood was more about constriction than shame, I think. Such a tight little rule-shaped life, on one hand. I did like the part about love, on the other hand. It was really big when I was in my teens. Pope John XXIII and all that good sixties lovin'. I was right in the middle of a revolution. I wish you could have been there, Aaron!

A

If I'd been alive in the sixties, I would have been alive in the fifties, too. And maybe the thirties and forties. V says there are endless copies of us across time and space, that whatever we imagine ourselves doing (and wherever we see ourselves doing it) it is happening. V is also addicted to Klonopin and goes through withdrawal at the end of every month because he takes too many pills early in the month. He got arrested once and kept saying *fuck the police* to the police. He has a cat named Pumpkin. Someone I know used to date him. Actually, they are still dating him, but if I write it in the past, then maybe it will be in the past. I guess, according to V, it is. And since we're talking about holy people, if V's right, does that mean Christ is being crucified

M

as I write this?

I'm glad crucifixion has changed over the centuries to cruci*fiction*. There is nothing more disturbing than coming upon someone hanging on a cross as you turn a corner in your quiet town on your way for muffins. I'm sure I will just have offended some people, and I apologize for that because I have nothing against muffins, truly, and I know some folks are pretty sensitive about them, and for good reason.

A

How to have unholy fun (both on and off a budget):
Fuck someone you know
(unwed). Fuck someone you don't
know and pay them well.

M

The problem with holiness is threefold:

1. It's non-theoretically impossible
2. It's theoretically boring
3. It's an idea that has lost all meaning

A

I like to joke during Easter:

> If Jesus rises from the grave and sees his shadow,
> we'll have six more weeks of winter.

Does it feel good to make unholy jokes because holiness was shoved so hard down some of our throats?

Here are some things that come in threes:

1) Primary colors
2) The three little pigs
3) Three French hens

4) The number of bones in the human ear
5) The Bronte sisters
6) Three-piece suits

7) Feet in a yard
8) Freud's theory of personality
9) Destiny's Child

10) Beetlejuice! Beetlejuice! Beetlejuice!
11) See no evil, hear no evil, speak no evil
12) The Fates

13) The rule of three
14) Rock, paper, scissors
15) Tercets

M

Rondelet for St. Sophia

As I write this
St. Sophia still stands, dazzling
In the sun. This
Is not a poem, this is fact.
She has stood for one thousand years,
My friends, one thousand fucking years.
She's the poem.

I think I like churches because they're quiet when you go there by yourself. When I was in high school I used to stop at St. Catherine of Siena's on my walk home from the bus stop. That was when my life was still ahead of me and everything I dreamed was fluffy as a cloud that could fit inside a church. It seemed

A

there were always so many things I dreamed
I could be, and the possibilities outweighed

the impossibilities, but I didn't know that then.
I remember once in my thirties walking 42nd

Street and seeing the marquees for the Broadway
musicals, thinking: *I'll never be a Broadway star.*

Not that I ever wanted to be, but I just knew
that possibility was gone. Those realizations

happen more and more each year. Before my
mom died, she told me: *most people in this life*

never get what they want. I think she meant: she
never got what she wanted, and some days

I'm not sure if I have or will or even know
what I want or have wanted anymore, but that

doesn't stop time does it, dear friend? Even
this poem will continue without us,

M

and maybe
and possibly
and perhaps

and occasionally
and sometimes
and once in a while

and rarely
and oddly
and hardly ever

this poem may actually
believe it or not
be

A

Holy (insert profanity of choice)

Good People

A

I say to my sister: *Maureen thinks we need another section because the book shouldn't end with Holy People* (amen to that), and I ask her for ideas of people we could write about. *Asshole People, Shitty People… You already have Sad People, right?* It's so unlike me, but I say: *I don't really want to end on a sad note. I mean, I don't need us to be cheerful, but I don't want to set us up for…well, you know, sadness. What about Good People*? She thinks about it: *I guess there are some good people left, not many, but some.*

M

I can't say this for certain, but I'm pretty sure I met two good people in Belvidere, New Jersey, when I was thirteen. They came into the Stone House at Johnson's Farm & Resort where my friend Kathy and I were listening to the jukebox and dancing around, having fun in the middle of the day. Two boys a couple of years older. They asked me to dance, one after the other, then left. Just me. Just like that. In a huge empty stone room with a jukebox. My friend said they were townies. I knew they were angels. I wish I could remember the song.

A

People are people, a throaty, old-soul woman said to me once. She was my sister's friend. We went to the car to get stoned, and she said that to me. I know it's cliché, but the *way* she said it, had lived it, made me hear it for the first time. The curtainy, hot-box smoke, the glowing world of that parking lot, and the dive bar we'd been drinking at, mothers dragging their kids into the grocery store for a gallon of milk: it was all so fucking gorgeous,

M

and I knew on that buzzy afternoon that those boys were good people and that I was a really good dancer. Until then it had only been me and the TV (*Bandstand*), where I learned quite young how to stroll, twist, cha-cha, and hand jive. The rest of my moves were something my Jersey parents handed down to me. Dancing—now there's one of the best things about people, don't you think? It might be one of the best parts about life itself.

Oh, and I danced with good men another time: on the pier over the Hudson, Gay Pride, nineties, when all was dark in NYC. Me and Lori and hundreds of giant gay guys around us as we danced, tiny and trying to keep up, among them. I couldn't believe how big they were. I couldn't believe I could feel so safe. And now I'm crying, of course.

A

I asked my barber in New York City why he thought
so many bald men tried comb-overs. They never look good,

I said, and he said, maybe they're shy. I loved him a little
then, even though he once nicked a mole on my scalp

and I walked down Avenue A with blood on my temple,
running down to my cheek. His name was Gregory.

He was from Russia. When I went back years later, he'd
sold the shop and moved to Arizona with the good, dry air.

He loved vodka. Blood and water and the green sterile liquid
they put the combs in to clean them between customers.

Sometimes the world is so liquid that it rushes through
each one of us and inside our chests are vast oceans.

He pronounced it *wodka*. Even that, dear friend, is beautiful.

I Put This Moment Over Here

after & for Kate Bush

I first heard Kate Bush in a smoky dorm room that one could
put on a postcard and send to their favorite god
on this planet or another planet or any of their favorite places
at the precise moment they're driving up that slick-ass road
over the river and through the woods (kidding). I'm afraid of icy hills
here, there, and everywhere, the slick simultaneity of building

confidence and fear, to get from here to somewhere, from one building
to another over labyrinths and holograms, oh, if only I could
freeze the best moments into "all the time," toss shit ones over the hill
like this worldwide one that seems to have enlisted every dark god.
A friend put "Wuthering Heights" on a mixtape for me before I hit the road,
and I replayed "The Big Sky" for 6 hours driving to Wyoming and other places

I'd always wanted to go and places I stumbled upon travel weary, places
put on maps by people hellbent on populating and cyber-building.
Does it all come to this: a lonely body in a scratched-up Ford on a twisty road,
the moment of rescue so far away (like lights on a bridge). I could—
I wish—step heart first over the bruised earth and hold the face of God
right here where there is so much that needs explaining, cities and hills

and telephone lines slicing the sky. Here, God, let's make a deal: this hill
overblown with dandelions and high with children is one of those places
where you, God, just for a moment, can strip off your mystery. Okay, God?
This is your chance to step up and perform at Woodstock '22, to build
an epic, symphonic encore in the bottom of our faithless guts. You could.
I would. If we swapped places. Me: You. You: a big old queer. The road—

my road—would sparkle like horses dipped in glitter and sequins. Your road
would put the whole lovely world back on the map, not plummet down the hill,
but if we can't have this (and we can't) do you think that maybe you could
take a moment to explain a few key things like why are all the beautiful places
overrun with un-beauty, or at least eclipsed by it, and why are we always building
here, there, everywhere, and up, upper, uppest as if trying to reach you? Hey, God,

we're down *here*. Why don't *you* reach *us* from your spaceship? Finally, God,
if you're ever over this way—between oceans or stars, or down the road
and you have a moment. Well, never mind. When I think how we've been building
it up, then tearing it all down, this gorgeous world, from mountain to molehill,
there's something I want to put in your god-sized ear: of all the places
you and I have co-created, this is the one I'd love for us to heal. If only we could.

A&M

All Things Go

after & for Sufjan Stevens

Carrie & Lowell. Is it terrible to start with an album considering all
the ways Sufjan interacts with the various gods and the way things
live both inside and outside us? But that is an album that always goes
flying off in death songs like lullabies or songs alight with death, and all
I want to do is just make out in my car. Remember those days when things
were the same as they are today (shaky) (wake me), yet we seemed to go

ahead with arrogant vulnerability, like a rock song strummed on a ukulele, go-
ing oblivious and playful one minute, cranky and hard-ass the next, all
etched on perfectly pressed vinyl or microphoned into everything?
I always wanted to sing myself but lacked the right hat and that thing
called talent and the ability to write perfect rhymes and melodies. I'm all
sung out today on the lip of Sufjan's sweet sound, itching to play or go

to Illinois and see all the sites that Sufjan names and serenades and then go
sign my name on one of three stars while playing the flute or maybe go
to Target or Walmart and buy feather pillows to make wings for us all.
The best part about Chicago after New York was going around gay, all
things gay, things gay friendly, things gay adjacent, things gay sexy, things
spread out like wings made out of pillows for a bunch of angels. So many things

can make a mortal man immortal and make love feel permanent, feel like things are just ducky and as long as we're queer we can get through anything, like going to the supermarket or hearing Sufjan sing about John Wayne Gacy—two things any straight human being would be shocked by, slain by. But there we go: queers craving the complicated, the undersides, the genuine and terrifying, all living on the sharp edges of a life we've been written into as if all things (all!)

concerning the UFO sighting near Highland, IL, are more important than all the movies with R. Gosling or baby geese in them put together. (Sorry.) Things Sufjan sings about: Tonya Harding, Ativan, video games, Vesuvius. Reall-
y, imagine you love Illinois, or any state, for that matter (he said he was going to make an album for each state, but then changed his mind). If I were going to go to Illinois, I would sing about Uncle Fun on Belmont and all the kitschy things

the owner discounted before he shut down and moved to Baltimore. The more things I can fit in my floor-to-ceiling bookcases, like Gumby & Gangsters & Ghosts & all the Guerrilla Girls art, the more I can high-note the love up from my toes, so it goes to show, to say, and to hope that there are at least a gillion gorgeous and glitzy things to make a person happy, okay if not happy, maybe joyful or awake or able to go to the Sears Tower with Sandburg on Pulaski Day. We're done. Finis. That's all.

Acknowledgments

Sincere thanks to the editors of the following publications in which some of the poems in this collection first appeared:

Cherry Tree: The sonnets beginning "Earring Magic Ken has his own Wikipedia page"; "When I'm sad, I sing in the car. When I'm happy"; "The first time I came across a bunch of rowdy lesbians"; "Listen up, queers of the world! There's something I've been meaning"; and "Here's the scoop for anyone who cares to know"

Court Green: "Leading Men"

The Massachusetts Review: "Rondelet for the Terminally Ill"

Poem-a-Day: "Sissy"

Under a Warm Green Linden: "All Things Go" and "I Put This Moment Over Here"

"The Sky Is an Elephant" appears in *Essential Queer Voices of U.S. Poetry* from Green Linden Press, Christopher Nelson, ed. It takes its inspiration from Jack Spicer and Federico García Lorca and, of course, Aaron Smith. It also appears in Maureen Seaton's final book, *The Sky Is an Elephant*; the poem "Rondelet for the Terminally Ill" appears in that book as well.

About the Authors

MAUREEN SEATON (1947-2023) authored twenty-three poetry collections, both solo and collaborative—most recently *The Sky Is an Elephant* (ELJ Editions, 2023); *Undersea* (Jackleg Press, 2021); and *Sweet World* (CavanKerry Press, 2019), winner of the Florida Book Award in Poetry. Her honors include Lambda Literary Awards for both lesbian memoir and lesbian poetry, the Audre Lorde Award, an NEA fellowship, and the Pushcart Prize. She was professor emerita of creative writing at the University of Miami and was voted Miami's Best Poet 2020 by the readers of the *Miami New Times*.

AARON SMITH is the author of five books published by the University of Pittsburgh Press's Pitt Poetry Series: *Stop Lying: Poems* (2023); *The Book of Daniel* (2019); *Primer* (2016); *Appetite* (2012); and *Blue on Blue Ground* (2005), winner of the Agnes Lynch Starrett Poetry Prize. He is a three-time finalist for the Lambda Literary Award and a two-time finalist for the Thom Gunn Award. He is a recipient of fellowships from the New York Foundation for the Arts and the Mass Cultural Council. With the poet James Allen Hall, he hosts *Breaking Form: a Poetry and Culture Podcast*. He is associate professor of creative writing at Lesley University in Cambridge, Massachusetts.

TILT

TILT

DENISE DUHAMEL
&
MAUREEN SEATON

BRIDWELL PRESS
Southern Methodist University
Dallas, Texas

Bridwell Press is the professional publishing arm of Bridwell Library
(SMU Libraries and Perkins School of Theology).
Southern Methodist University

SMU Libraries SMU Perkins School of Theology

Design by Alicia Beebe

Printed in the United States of America

ISBN: 978-1-957946-21-4 (hardback)
ISBN: 978-1-957946-22-1 (paperback)
ISBN: 978-1-957946-24-5 (epub)

Cover image: *Girl with Alpaca* by Joshua Benmore

If Earth were not tilted, the amount
of light a given location receives would be fixed,
and there would be no seasons.

ENCYCLOPEDIA BRITANNICA

for Emily & Jennifer

Contents

Introduction

Here's a little bit about the wonderful Maureen Seaton (1947–2023).

Maureen was born in Elizabeth, New Jersey. Throughout her life she lived in many places, including Long Island; Chicago; New York City; Hollywood, Florida; and Longmont, Colorado, where she passed away. She authored fifteen solo books of poetry, the last of which was *The Sky Is an Elephant*, published only months before her death. *Furious Cooking* (1996) won the Iowa Poetry Prize. *Sweet World* (2019) won the Gold Medal Florida Book Award for Poetry. She published fourteen co-authored books of poetry before she passed and this book is the fifteenth, making her poetry publications half solo and half collaborative. Maureen was a Libra, so I think she'd like this even split. Her memoir *Sex Talks to Girls* (2008) earned her a Lambda Literary Award. In fact, her awards and honors were many, including residencies at Ragdale, Ucross, and the Devils Tower National Monument. She received a National Endowment for the Arts fellowship, an Illinois Arts Council Grant, a Pushcart Prize, and Publishing Triangle's Audre Lorde Award. As befitting an advocate for poetry as well as the gay community, in 2018 she co-edited (with Neil de la Flor) *Reading Queer: Poetry in a Time of Chaos*.

Maureen was also a born teacher. I never saw someone delight so much in introducing poetry to students. One of the reasons she went to get her MFA (from Vermont College, 1994–1996) was so that she could teach full time. She'd already published two books when she was accepted into that program, yet she delighted in telling me about all she was learning. She was

a beloved professor at the Art Institute and Columbia College, both in Chicago. She was hired at the University of Miami in 2002 to teach in the MFA program and even became director. She retired in 2020, due to her illness. If she had her way (i.e., had her health), she would have kept going.

Maureen, the matriarch of her family, had two incredible daughters, two incredible sons-in-law, and a grandson Mikey. She and her partner Lori were together since 1992. She also leaves behind many poetry friends and fans. I am but one of them.

And now here's a little bit about how Maureen and I came to collaborate.

In the spring of 1987, I gave a reading at Sarah Lawrence College in New York, from which I'd soon graduate with my MFA. Maureen was living in Tarrytown, near the school, and happened to stop by. After the event, we talked everything poetry. She seemed so knowledgeable and worldly to me. She was working at the time as an assistant poetry editor at the *Croton Review*, which I found very glamorous. We went on a picnic the following weekend and were best friends thereafter. We shared our solo poems with each other for the next three years. Maureen had studied with Marilyn Hacker at the 92nd Street Y and was writing mostly sonnets. I was writing free verse and prose poems.

Then, in 1990, I went to hear the poet David Trinidad give a reading at the St. Mark's Poetry Project. David asked his friend Bob Flanagan to join him on stage to read some of their collaborations from their chapbook *A Taste of Honey*. I was hooked! The next morning I called Maureen and explained as best I could what I had witnessed… *Want to try this?* I asked her, reading poems from *A Taste of Honey* to her. And it was my good fortune that she was up for it.

When we began, we had no idea about the surrealist tradition that encouraged collaboration. All we could think to do was skip along, one line after the other. I felt more comfortable opening the poem, so I usually did. Maureen loved wrapping up poems, so that became her forte. Maureen had recently moved from Tarrytown to the Bronx, and I was in Chelsea. Since we were both working several jobs to support ourselves, we couldn't spend whole days writing. Instead, what we did most often was leave each other lines on our answering machines. We had a blast! I remember Maureen quoting Carl Jung, "The creation of something new is not accomplished by intellect but by the play instinct acting from inner necessity." Maureen and I engaged in some serious play.

We must have written thirty or forty one-line-at-a-time poems when Maureen came across *The Book of Surrealist Games* describing Exquisite Corpse, a method in which writers compose two lines of poetry at a time and then fold the paper in such a way that each writer can only see half of the lines her partner has written. Maureen and I started playing. We wrote our lines on paper and sent them through the mail. We eventually adapted the game so that we could still play by leaving our lines as phone messages. Once we both had email—circa 1995—we adapted once more, sending each other just half the lines we wrote and filling each other in on the missing lines when the poem was "done," which usually meant we had reached the line quota we set for ourselves before beginning to write.

As time went on, we grew bolder in our experiments. We made Exquisite Corpse sonnets, sestinas, pantoums, villanelles, and centos. She encouraged me to embrace traditional forms, while I introduced her to prose poetry and free verse—and those collaborative impulses influenced our solo work as well. (Maureen's 2018 book *Fisher*, for example, is a book of prose poems. Traditional forms persist in my work.) After those early days of collaboration

in New York, Maureen moved to Chicago and we continued our collaborations by email and writing visits. Then, in the early 2000s, we both wound up living in Florida, four miles apart. Maureen was teaching at the University of Miami and I at Florida International University, where I still teach today. Sometimes we wrote by the ocean. In 2004, we rode out Hurricane Charley together and wrote poems by candlelight after losing power. We delighted in creating a third voice, a voice that was neither Maureen's nor mine, but rather some poetic hybrid. Maureen described this voice as "restless, goofy, shrill—basically unbecoming to a woman. Sometimes it is easier for us to be unbecoming together." I agree—there was a boldness in our collaborations even though Maureen was already a brave solo poet.

Maureen and I were deep in poetic collaboration, learning as much as we could. We teamed up with David Trinidad to edit *Saints of Hysteria: A Half-Century of Collaborative American Poetry* (Soft Skull Press, 2007). We gathered collaborative poems by the Beats, New York School poets, feminist poets of the 1970s and '80s, the Naropa Poets, the Unbearable Poets of the Lower East Side, L=A=N=G=U=A=G=E poets, and more "mainstream" poet-pairs like Jim Harrison & Ted Kooser, Maggie Anderson & Lynn Emanuel, Stephen Dunn & Lawrence Raab, and Joshua Beckman & Matthew Rohrer. We discovered the impulse to collaborate had been there all along! But because many of the poems we found appeared in literary magazines or small-press chapbooks, these experiments were hidden like tree frogs, only to be found once we knew how to spot them.

Maureen and I were lucky in that we were able to get our poems published in book and pamphlet form. *Exquisite Politics*, in which Maureen and I explore sexual politics, came out in 1997 from Tia Chucha Press. Our chapbook *Oyl* (Pearl Editions, 2000) recasts Popeye's paramour, making her the plucky protagonist. (Maureen had an obsession with Olive Oyl and collected

OO memorabilia.) In our chapbook *Little Novels* (Pearl Editions, 2002) we boil the canon down to sonnet-sized tales highlighting secondary or disenfranchised characters. *Caprice: Collaborations—Collected, Uncollected, and New* was published by Sibling Rivalry Press in 2015. And another chapbook *Questionnaire for Two Pussies* was released by Virgin Press in 2021.

Maureen was diagnosed with cancer in 2014. When her metastatic diagnosis came in 2017, she moved to Colorado to live with her daughter, son-in-law, and grandson. Though Maureen was often sick for stretches at a time, whenever she emerged with energy she was ready to collaborate. She collaborated not only with me but also with Aaron Smith (switch this book over and you can read *Beautiful People*). Her other collaborative partners included Neil de la Flor, Kristine Snodgrass, Nicole Tallman, Carolina Hospital, Nicole Hospital-Medina, and Holly Iglesias. She also made guest appearances in books by the troika of poets Jeffery Conway, Gillian McCain, and David Trinidad. My go-to joke was that she and I had an "open poetry relationship."

The majority of poems in *Tilt* were written during Maureen's illness, post 2014. We used a variety of techniques as we went along. "Credo" is a substitution-filled riff on "The Apostle's Creed." (Maureen and I both grew up Catholic.) "12 Lines about Gender (Florida-style)," "12 Lines about Gender (the Cosmos)," and "12 Lines about Gender (Retro)" are all mini-sonnets. The end words that appear are genders Maureen was asked to choose from on a form she was filling out. *Tilt* was a departure for us, as we loosened what we thought of as a sonnet—sometimes discarding the end rhymes we'd worked so hard to get right in earlier books, though "Number's Up" called back to that stricter, more traditionally formal approach. We amused ourselves writing "Heroic"—Maureen was a good sport about that pandemic-inspired sonnet sequence, indulging my fascination with talk-show host Wendy Williams. She said it was only fair, as I was not dissuaded by her

preoccupation with Olive Oyl. We wrote this poem two lines at a time, going back-and-forth by email.

Some of Maureen's illness coincided with the pandemic, and the fourth section of *Tilt* is situated during this time. Other gestures new to our collaborations are the terza rima and abecedarian. Coming together to write terza rima ("Equinox" and "Solstice") gave us the formal rigor that we had previously reserved for our sonnets. For these two companion poems, we each wrote one stanza at a time, setting up the rhyme scheme for each other as we alternated. The abc-poems ("'A is for Alpha' & Other Axed Sesame Street Songs" and "Songs of Hierarchy & Hoodie") and their variations ("Howl" and "Death Is Not a Riddle") felt like coming back to the basic building blocks of language, as we knew we'd be saying goodbye soon. We also used the title of the improv game "Yes, And," a nod to how deliciously improvisational our collaborations had become over the years.

How lucky am I to have had this creative friendship with Maureen. The anthropologist Gregory Bateson coined the phrase "it takes two to know one," a twisting of the cliché "it takes one to know one," a mean-spirited and childish retort often heard on playgrounds in response to an insult. Bateson believed that, just as animal and plant species were dependent upon one another and shared an intelligence, humans were also capable of creating a collective self that "thinks." This is how it was writing with Maureen. It was singing, it was playing, it was thinking. And it did indeed take two!

Denise Duhamel, Hollywood, Florida
July 2024

Credo

We believe in one gorgonzola,
   the cracker, the almond;
in all cheeses, floral and herbaceous,
   complex, creamy, & crumbly.

We believe in one quiche Lorraine,
   the brunch of all brunches,
pie of all pies, savory and loaded
   with bacon, onions, & nutmeg,

truly homemade crust with butter
   and a rolling pin, not frozen,
and a silky center. We believe
   in the mango on its tree of life.

Through its juices all things,
   all things are made,
all love restored, all thirst quenched
   in its sweet deliciousness

as though the very branch
   it grew upon was heaven
and all creation waits faithfully below
   to catch it when it falls.

§

Holy Hippocampus: A Conversation in Couplets

The human brain stores a million gigabytes of memory, so why is it
I can't recall where I plunked down my keys or orange flash drive?

If only I could access the words of Proust I read at twenty or what
you said yesterday about how to treat a cold—was it frankincense?

Frank remembers you so clearly but you can't access his face even
looking at his picture. High school classmates, grade school teachers:

a blur! I've always wanted to tell you that my mother with Alzheimer's
recalled her Carteret childhood in encyclopedic detail—but that was it.

Did she forget being a mother and your childhood? I love reimagined
retro postcards: *I left my baby on the bus*! Or *I forgot to have children.*

That's my mom! Unable to spell *world* backwards by fifty-five. *d-l-*
r-o-w. They say the brain alters a memory simply by remembering it.

That is why I remember my second-grade accordion as gold
but in pictures it is maroon. In one my hair has a green tint—impossible,

or ahead of your time, as always! They also say our short-term memory
holds only seven pieces of information at a time. Holy Hippocampus!

Number 8: *Where did I park my car?* nudges out Conan O'Brien's punch
line and whether or not I turned off the coffeepot. My remote key beeps,

but the kid who insisted on pushing my grocery cart is telling me where
he snowshoes (9), my cell's ringing in the surreal distance of some pocket

in my jacket or purse or reusable tote and I fear someone I love
is in trouble—an accident, a broken heart, a bounced check. *Hello?*

My brain needs an upgrade. Higher resolution for those misty
water-colored tidbits that pixilate rebelliously as I furrow my brow.

What I do remember is Bert's chalk sidewalk drawing turning
into a painting when it rained. Or was it Mary Poppins' magic?

I know you're not thinking I'd remember a movie I only saw five times,
are you? What about that annoying link between memory and hormones?

Or that stress kills memory cells? I read that doing certain tasks
can stimulate the growth of brain cells, but I can't remember which tasks.

Well, we're both good at math! Today I read that it takes the brain 80
milliseconds to process info. For that time we're actually living in the past.

Pomp & Pyrotechnics

I used to believe in numerology and astrology charts, a tarot
reading now and then. Once the future was a mysterious soup

of possibilities I slurped on New Year's Eve as balls fell
and rockets red-glared over tremulous worldwide cities

of neon and Nembutal. I was sure everything "happened
for a reason," which irritated my cynical friends. Reason,

that glitzy show-off, partner of rhyme and rationale, waiting
beside me like a date, all dressed up and giddy with faith.

I tried New Age and once I thought I was slain by a minister
who cured my asthma for a day. Then the miasma of New York,

the thrill of all those bodies banging into and off each other
above ground and below, that grand soul rush to prosperity.

This is the line of the poem where I expect it should turn—
But now I believe… What about you? Do you believe in

poetry? What if, turning, the poem runs smack into a wall
glorious with graffiti in neighborhoods we never knew existed?

Poor poem, flattened like a boring interoffice memo, the ones
I have taken pride in ignoring most of my life. What if

poems and memos (almost anagrams) carry the same weight
after all, like stars (*Chloë Sevigny)* and stars *(Sirius A)?*

While I don't believe in sister wives, I do believe in Dog Stars—
or is it the other way around? I consult my star map and find

my face projected like Pepper's ghost all over the cosmos.
I'm astral, subatomic, hold my breath and pass through stuff.

O, 2019, please be kind to us—by us, I mean the poets
making this poem and everyone else who wants to believe

or couldn't care less about the pomp and pyrotechnics
of a world to which we're all born, perishable and dreamy-eyed.

Number's Up

There are two galaxies for everyone alive,
over seven quintillion grains of sand,
one rich man squinting from a needle's eye,
two poor gals, arms linked in an ampersand.

Thriving hives hold thirty-thousand bees,
the Powerball jackpot, a cool billion.
A year's the record for the longest sneeze.
The rainforest's eighty percent Brazilian.

One in four people cannot smell cyanide.
One in four people cannot taste bitter food.
Each day people talk to themselves six times.
One out of ten stand-up comics are booed.

Now they say that time has no beginning,
though Earth's at the bottom of its ninth inning.

"A is for Alpha" & Other Axed Sesame Street Songs

A is tops, alpha, a known quantity in algebra,
but why? Why is bush-league B always second to
cousins who can't cut equal corners of cake for C, and
doesn't D deserve all the deliciousness of real dairy
even when Ethan Hawke insists D remain a vegan?
Forget the hierarchy of the Food Network, forget
gastronomy and gourmet or any of the ghastly
hegemonic and homo-ironic horror hits
inciting irritation! I, for one, am an insurgent,
juggling joy and Jurassic extinction at Jiffy Lube.
Kick me. Or kick a Rockette. I love the letter K!
Love when those la la's and lampposts and lightbulbs
morph into monarchs and blue morpho butterflies.

Never mind the inadvertent narrator who knows
one is only in it for the story. Or the octopus. Oh,
Pluto knows me better than you, Pansy Popular.
Quickest to the crime scene at Quality Inn, you
resuscitated the robber whose acid reflux rendered him
Sid or Nancy. Either way, someone shady saved
the least popular letter, T, and there you totally go.
Univision's movie version *Pansy y Nancy* was
voted most likely to sequel. Verily, verily, I say
WTF? Sometimes I say: Mrs. Wiggins, why wait for
Xfinity when finity is so x-otic on its own?
Yin yearns for Yang in a New York yellow cab
zigzagging traffic, their hands at each other's zippers.

Songs of Hierarchy & Hoodie

Z zeroes in on me in my nightmare, my ZZZ's
yanked away by my own yelps. But youngsters
X-Men their way out of xylophonic wars, don't they?
What? White? Who wants to know? Your best friend
Vimeo-ed the vagaries of vagabonds vandalizing
umpteen Uber cars driven by university undergrads
tripping on Toll House. Tsk. Now a testy taskmaster
steals shindigs and slaloms down Sacagawea's
road, racing by rodeos, roundups, and ranch hands
quoting Raymond Queneau—"this queer fish was quite bats."
Perhaps Popeye or perhaps Philadelphia. Perhaps
oscillate or on occasion ossify. Olive Oyl too, only
new to Noam Chomsky, never nonchalant.

Memorials accommodate each 9mm's mistake,
like our land's a land of laws, not justice, whoops, don't
kid about the letter J, we're not there yet, kiddo—
just between us, justice is a joke in the 24 Jacksons
in the US, in Ferguson, in Inglewood. Injustice is
howl not hoot, hobble not help, Holy Hitman,
G., grab gossamer, rabid guns are for ghosts
freaking out about their finality, floating for-
ever on the edges of the equinox of epiphany.
Dear Doris Day and Dalai Lama, please do not deliver
carloads of *que seras* to the kids on the corner.
Bodyguard them from bullies and bullets, be
airtight angels adept at ascendance and assistance.

§

12 Lines about Gender (Florida-style)

I looked to the sky, UFO above me, or was it a gender
rolling over and over in that big sky like a female
orgasm, delirious with flashing lights? Intercoastal intersex
is so lovely with its salt water and its fresh: true Two-Spirit
brackishness. I mistook a manatee for an androgynous
goddess of rising sea and sinking city, gender-fluid
silver ripples along her back. I spied an omega male
kayaking quietly through musky mangroves, all genderqueer
with their gorgeous underwater roots, their agenda agender
and big love (the nursery of the world!). One transgender
spaceship (or was it a cloud?) was tired of cisgender
sand hogs and sea bullies and wrote across the sky: *Bye, Gender!*

12 Lines about Gender (the Cosmos)

I believe there is no one on the planet luckier than a bi-gender,
who, like a hipster trickster, lives above the fray, unidentifiable
in their lovely/lanky/stunning/staggering way beyond cisgenders
and their scripts. Monday I'm a femme, Tuesday, androgynous
as a moon pouring light in a cosmos that's so gender-fluid
it holds Castor, Pollux (twin boys), and Venus (so female,
she's star of both morning and evening, leading the sun, male,
and earthly Gillette to name a razor in her honor). Agender
ex-planet, Pluto, boasts five moons of mythical transgendered
radiance. Astronomists spy on Nix, its interstellar intersex
moonstruck self, as they fly by Pluto to confirm its two-spirit
orbit. The Hubble zooms in on each lovely sphere, genderqueer.

12 Lines about Gender (Retro)

When I was in high school, no one knew the word genderqueer
would be walking the halls hand in hand with the word bi-gender
trading lip gloss and rainbow suspenders with gender-fluid
cheerleaders and soccer players we all assumed were cisgender
until Halloween when they were ghosts or elves, androgynous,
or dressed up as a whole new gender (boo!) not yet identified.
No one knew Victoria's Secret Valentina Sampaio, first transgender
supermodel, would win so many hearts or influence so many male
heteros who ogled her, asking themselves, "What is a gender
supposed to do when the world is expanding into spirits?"
No one knew back then how expansive the word female,
how *American Pie* was American pi, the levee overflowing.

14 Lines about Water

Brooke Shields and a monster hail from lagoons
while Bridget Fonda rows anything but placid on a lake
searching for a croc. In the lead pipes of Flint,
water dies in kids' cups and bubbles of stagnant
pre-bedtime routines. A girl who's never seen the sea
gets caught in a rip and curls inside its weedy womb,
its House of Secrets, where the Swamp Thing swamps
and the Goddess of Sunken Ships reveals her briny
anchor. She wears a necklace of shells, a choppy
grin that glows phosphorescent in cans of seltzer.
We never believed there could be so much rain,
but the way the world is drowning at low tide
makes us rash—diving into strangers' swimming pools,
dumping jugs of H2O as our children cross the desert.

13 Lines about Walls

Frost: *Something there is that doesn't love a wall.*
Joyce: *and how he kissed me under the Moorish wall.*
A wallflower, I peeked at Mr. Popular leaning against a brick wall.
Wallowing, I wept for Ms. Popular as if desire were a wall-
paper pattern Charlotte Perkins Gilman traced decades before Stonewall.
What? Have we all become proverbial balls to some caterwauling wall
of fake news? After each hurricane, I replace the drywall
as if any wall stands a chance against nature. What's a wall
but a makeshift "fuck you," waves walloping the seawall
like walleyes bent on survival? Some walls are metaphorical walls
in the mind of a tyrant who promises a nation concrete walls.
Cavafy: *Ah why did I not pay attention when they were building the walls.*
Emerson: *Murder will speak out of stone walls.*

§

Equinox

Pictures of the virus are pretty—
like sea creatures or pin-cushioned moons
or holograms posing in semi-witty

situations beside balls and balloons
glowing with coronas, crowns, halos.
Under microscopes, *SpongeBob* cartoons

look fractal-similar, my own lungs aglow
with pink rods and blue cones. I'm silly
then scared. Neighbors hoard Purell, ammo

against infection. I try to chill, be
a peaceful citizen, a good locked-up
or locked-down member of society.

I'm "Baking Bad," filling measuring cups
to make pot brownies for frantic friends
and a wedding cake for Sam & Sonny's nup-

tials, virtual and queer and legal and
euphoric. We'll each dance in our Zoom box
to the host's boombox, no need to pretend

we're anywhere but in our PJs and socks,
our pink boas and perky blue face masks
(lest we're contagious). It's the equinox,

night and day perfectly split. Sam basks
in Sonny, Sonny in Sam, a perfect fit.
Then the day goes back to quarantined tasks—

hand washing (my fingers so dry!), chit-
chatting on my Clorox-wiped iPhone,
bombarding heaven for the sad and the sick.

Solstice

Stonehenge is closed this solstice. Pagans,
druids, and tourists can watch online
or create their own backyard haven

of ancient megalithic stones, or find
solace in gobbling up strawberries
or building a Classic LEGO shrine.

The day will be long. No need to worry
about time or whether or not the sun
in your natal chart is in Aries.

Priests will baptize babies with squirt guns,
amen, while at-risk oldsters line up
to be shot with Holy Oil and sent "home." Fun

fact: more people are using their Krups
single-serve coffee makers these days.
Plus fish are used as spies now—guppies,

grouper, jellyfish—to keep our seas safe
from Russia, Iran, China, Iraq,
or whoever we fear most. Gamma rays

are invisible yet still wreak havoc
on the human body. This summer solstice,
check your noontime shadow as you walk,

see how tiny you are as you cross this
crazy Earth, how everything's so stark raving
bright you can hardly believe you exist.

This Different Life

3.22.20

MS: *What is it like for you to walk by the sea now, my friend?*

DD: The sea is roped off by yellow caution tape and orange barricades, the colors reminding me of jellyfish that sometimes wash up to the shore, that I sometimes mistake for toys. Police cars patrol the bike lane, no sirens but red lights flashing atop. We can no longer walk on the sand or step to the water to test its temperature—it was so cold in early March, last time I checked. I'm hoping the sea is getting her rest without our sunblock, our water bottles and other trash, without so many flights dumping fuel, without so many cruise ships. When my grandnephews were here in February, they made a game of picking up not only shells, but popsicle sticks, beer can pop-tops, a flip-flop, and straws. They were proud of each find, the garbage going into the trash, the shells going back to the shore.

3.23.20

DD: *My friend, what is it like for you to walk with your all-terrain walker in the park?*

MS: Yesterday I took my ATV (aka, walker) to the Sawhill Ponds trailhead in the shadow of the Rockies (our parks have trails here, in and out of foothills, around lakes and along creeks that crash over waterfalls). I took a deep breath and headed down the trail. The mountains are still open here. They rise over Boulder, snow-laden and staunch. But to the north, Rocky Mountain National Park closed down a few days ago and you could hear the geese in Sawhill Pond loudly discussing the closure. Those geese—definitely not keeping a six-foot distance from each other or the ducks. Some people say closing the great park will give animals a chance to enjoy it for a change. I like that, although there I was, inching along on my ATV, grabbing up the open space for myself.

3.24.20

MS: *After Hurricane Wilma in 2005 there was a 10 p.m. curfew on Hollywood Beach. Have you got one now?*

DD: No curfews for us yet in Hollywood, but just south, Sunny Isles Beach has one in place. Maybe I should go outside tonight and stand in the dark while I can? I've become a creature of a makeshift routine, taking my walk at 5 or so every day when the streets are the least crowded, buildings providing the most shade. Because of my skin's tendency to burn rather than tan, I get a mole check every year. The doctor who examined me on March 12 told me I had to take the virus seriously, stay in place and not fly. She was not making a suggestion, but rather a mandate. Though much has changed, the sea turtles have come back as they do each March, starting to lay their eggs. Though much has changed, the city has dimmed the streetlights like they always do. No markers or cones around the nests. No beachgoers to accidentally step on them.

3.25.20

DD: *What's it like being a home-schooling art teacher to Sebby?*

MS: It seems so strange that the sea turtles are coming and going without people getting in their way for once, sending them off-course, leading them to mini malls. Is it okay if I talk about turtles for a minute rather than my grandson, who is six and loves going to homeschool during shelter-in-place because he pretty much gets to do just what he wants? Especially in art class! I found a dead baby turtle once up in Jensen Beach where my parents had moved because they loved the loggerheads. It seemed like a toy to me, lying there on the sand, or at least a souvenir. I wanted to show it to someone, but the beach was empty and it was late, so I buried it before I headed home. Honestly, it was an amazing day for me. Something wild in the palm of my hand. It was too late to save it, but not too late to grieve.

3.26.20

MS: *Carl Jung might say our collective shadow has reared up before us. What do you think about the photo of the fox asleep on a tree stump that went viral this week?*

DD: The fox represents erratic, unpredictable behavior. The fox represents going it alone. The fox represents seclusion and reflection. The fox can be sneaky, maybe someone is telling you a lie. The fox is all these things, according to my dream dictionary. Jung believed in the archetype of the trickster, like the fox, who appears to disrupt the natural order. To quote Carl: *The creative mind plays with the objects it loves.* We are writing, playing with the things we love—turtles, geese, jellyfish, and ducks. Now the fox which makes me think of trickster Fox News, a channel I refuse. Better to look to an orange sleeping fox if I want to make something up. Poor tree stump, a life cut short.

3.27.20

DD: *Can you believe, on the Italian island of Sardinia, dolphins have come back in the absence of ferries?*

MS: I will believe anything about dolphins. I remember them from my sixtieth birthday when I was already old enough to catch this virus, but not too old to swim with dolphins, and I wrote a poem about them and my friend Jeannette and how she swam with them once and they kept pushing her to the side of the pool and scaring her a little which is not like dolphins usually but it turns out they liked her a lot and she told me to be careful when I was swimming with them and I was. Whenever I see one, either in person or in recent videos about Sardinia or Venice, the cells in my body glow, I can actually feel my cells remembering they are alive and no matter how terrifying the world may be there are dolphins somewhere waiting to come back to us.

3.28.20

MS: *Do you find that food tastes different suddenly? I know everything is more precious now—a pound of meat has to last; bread's gone missing from the grocery store shelves. But what about the way it all tastes?*

DD: I remember the first time I saw "dolphin" on the menu in Florida and I gasped in horror, not realizing it was another name for mahi-mahi. I haven't had fish since March 10 when I had one of those long days at school—two thesis defenses and a class. I had a break in the middle and went to get sushi! I so seldom go to restaurants alone, but now, with shelter-in-place, for days on end I am eating alone. Food tastes Technicolor, though I am eating the same things. Oatmeal, hummus, chicken strips all pop in my mouth! And I have added one treat. I sometimes order takeout from Angelo's, the restaurant at the condo, that only has one or two offerings a day. Twice I have ordered a Greek salad because it's served with two warm garlic rolls, nestled like twins in foil. When I unwrap them I think of that old cliché—now I can die happy.

3.29.20

DD: *What is the most surprising thing you've found so far as you unpack your boxes from storage in Florida? Was there anything you forgot about? Was there anything you see now that you don't remember at all?*

MS: Everything feels like a surprise! I stuck my hand in a manilla envelope yesterday, touched hair, and let out a little scream. Everyone looked up from what they were doing and I pulled out a great mass of auburn hair about a foot long. Mine. But I don't know from when or where. I think the how is that I once asked a haircutter to cut it all off, starting at the rubber band at the base of my neck. It was LONG, Jack! And I do remember a time when I thought of donating my hair to an organization that makes wigs for women on chemo. Yesterday I was going to throw it away because there is not one person in my family who wants it! But I think I shall keep it just in case I need a wig myself. Right? (For a few minutes just now I forgot about the virus. It feels wrong, somehow, like I cheated on everyone. For a minute, it was just me, you, and my creepy/gorgeous red hair.)

3.29.20

MS: *The other night I went to a Zoom meeting and all the women were really relaxed. One was lying down. One had her dog beside her. The interesting thing to me was that everyone's hair was a lot messier than I remember (in our other life). How about your hair, Denise?*

DD: I love the image of your foot-long hair sample! I'm so glad you are saving it, as it has been with you all this time. I remember when you had long straight hair—it was always (and still is!) so shiny. I asked you once what kind of shampoo you used and after you told me, said, *honestly, it's probably just my genetics*. These days my own hair is in tangles! And it feels such a relief just to say so. I had my last appointment to get my roots done on March 9—what luxury, that former life. I have a small halo (a corona, you could say) of gray now and I have thought about what I will do when it gets out of hand. (Talk about shallow!) I am wearing my hair now almost exclusively in two braids, which seems the best way to keep it somewhat in place when I take my walks. Stray hairs still sometimes tickle in the wind, and I know we aren't supposed to touch our faces. When I feel the urge to scratch, I force up my sunglasses as a makeshift headband. When I Zoomed for work on Friday, I did comb my hair out and wore earrings and a nice shirt. From my waist down, which no one could see, were a ratty pair of yoga pants. When we cleaned out my mother's drawers, my sister and I each found a curl of our little girl hair she'd saved. Mine was so blond it was almost white, the color I hope my hair will return to if I live long enough.

3.30.20

DD: *Is there anything you used to be worried about that has floated away now that we are living this different life?*

MS: Well, I used to worry that I would miss teaching too much if I retired. Then I worried that I would miss my house in Miami if I moved to Colorado. Then I worried that I will never be able to dance again because my L3 splintered into a million pieces and when I try to dance I fall down. I worried that a lot of people in this country are more stupid than I could ever imagine. Then I worried that I will die of the virus instead of cancer. At that point, I started laughing. I'm laughing all the way to your house by the sea. I'm six feet away from you right now.

Heroic

As a surgery girl, you save money,
you plan for years. Then all of a sudden
corona pops up, and you've got to deal
with these saggy boobs. Poor Wendy Williams—
alcoholism, despicable ex-
husband. Rich Wendy driving a Rolls-Royce.
In fact, corona popping up like that
has put dampers on totally safe and
necessary things, one spokesperson
for The Time Before the Rumored Virus
spit into his megaphone, right before
handing it to Gramps, the designated
hitter, who asked *Who wants bacon?* The crowd
chanted *Open Tyson! Open Tyson!*

Meanwhile, the Tyson plant remains quite closed
as the workers wait and the hogs wait and
Americans who need bacon wait wait
wait. Today I couldn't wait so I sliced
a tomato, washed some lettuce, slathered
mayo on toast and pretended it was
a BLT from the Lower East Side
Coffee Shop. O, New York, with your jam-packed
tenements and F train, we did have us
some good times, didn't we? Kissing strangers,
tagging walls with neon spray paint—*Slumlord!*
Now swings in Tompkins Square Park are empty
and I've been missing you for thirty years.
Get well soon, Broadway and Christopher Street.

In the '80s, Broadway, Christopher Street,
and Brooklyn came alive in Keith Haring's
Soho Pop Shop. He made *A Pile of Crowns*,
an elegy for his friend Basquiat,
and iconic buttons: "Stop AIDS Worldwide."
Who will draw this pandemic? Make sense of
why the only ones psychotic enough
to write about the beauty of the word
corona are the poets? *Corona,*
coronal, coronation, coroner.
I can't believe the color of the sky
right now. Blue. As if the day is normal.
Sea turtles still bury eggs. In two months
a group of hatchlings will dig themselves out.

Baby loggerheads still dig themselves up
and out of those chilly Atlantic sands
and head toward the toasty Gulf Stream waters.
I wonder who will emerge from our own
live burial and who will hightail it
to the boardwalk's lights or back to the sea?
Me! Me! I think, wanting nothing more than
to dance at Margaritaville's band shell
with my sister, drunk tourists, toddlers, teens,
the homeless, all swaying equal under
the moon. But will I be too scared? Will I
hesitate before the sand, the sea foam?
Will everything I've known myself to be
push me forward into uncharted life?

Remember Dolittle's Pushmi-Pullyu,
with one head that ate, another that talked?
The creature's great-grandfather was the last
unicorn, or so the Doctor believed.
Scientists rush for a vaccine so we don't
go the way of the quagga or dodo.
Speaking of endangered birds (the dodo?),
my daughter (our go-to-stores heroine)
came home with six baby chicks yesterday.
Maybe not endangered yet, but awfully cute,
and a way to self-sustain if the bug
keeps rampaging o'er the plains and Rockies.
Quarantine souffles! Stay-at-home omelets!
In Florida, the go-to is Grubhub.

In Colorado, our governor's gay,
a Democrat, a Jew, which has nothing
to do with how we order our take-out,
but I want to believe him when he sounds
so hopeful I can almost imagine
eating at The Roost on Main in August.
In Florida, our governor's racist,
a Republican, which has everything
to do with opening up too early
though I want to be hopeful too that when
he buys Mother's Day presents at Rusted
Arrow he's tender, transformed, loves us all.
Wait up! Do politicians really have
mothers at home praying them out of hell?

The father of Florida's governor
said of Obama—he's a "cop-hating
terrorist." So there's that. I try not to
rage, as stress hinders our immune systems.
My audio died on my TeleMed
visit so my doc used the chat function.
Then TeleMed died completely and we
ended up on cell phones. (Bye, Doc, stay safe.)
I told a friend that nothing is worse than
giving birth, but this is so much longer,
this waiting for the midwife while sucking
ice chips. Speaking of fathers, where the hell
are they? Shouldn't they be giving piggy-
back rides? The kids have outgrown their sneakers.

Ah, the kids are outgrowing their childhoods
as we write sonnets, but who wants to be
a prophet? Apple News Spotlight: How
New Zealand eliminated the virus
plus easy ways to decorate without
spending a goddam dime. (Profanity
is the new black. Everyone's embracing
the f-bomb.) Emma Byrne wrote a whole book
about the virtues of swearing and how
transgressing polite speech can actually
help us tolerate pain and promote trust
in teamwork. Toddlers say "doo doo head" when
the urge hits to fight back. Personally,
as prophets, we say "doo doo head of state."

The president loves profit, doo-wopping
with the Senate, off-key and out of touch.
Alice (who's five) said, "He's going to blow
up the world." When her mother asked, "What?"
Alice laughed, "Don't worry. He's not even
real" and returned to her LEGO tower.
Not T—'s Tower, of course. Something more fun,
like Mia's Tree House or Olivia's
Cupcake Café. Remember the guy who
used suction cups to climb from the 5th floor
to the 21st? And remember when
T— lobbied against sprinklers? What's with that?
Too cheap to install them! Then his tenant
died in a fire on the 50th floor.

Now we've had more deaths in our fifty states
than there are 4th magnitude fiery
supernovas in the night sky. Look up
between Boötes and Hercules—
you might glimpse the Northern Crown (Corona
Borealis) sparkling far above Earth.
The astrologist Susan Miller blames
Pluto, which rules finances, viruses,
and masses of people. Albert Einstein's fake quote:
There are only two ways to live your life.
One, as though nothing is a miracle.
The other, as though everything is…
Today is Mother's Day. There's a woman
on her knees across the street planting roses.

I'm on my knees, saying the rosary,
when I forget what comes after bead four,
"Glory Be." I'm praying for my mother
in the nursing home and all the patients
who've tested positive. Rather than look
it up, I decide to pray freestyle—O,
Mary, full of grace and able to leap
tall politicians in a single bound,
please put in a good word for my mother
and all mothers, especially the ones
who are alone today. Hold their hands, calm
their fears. Let them know they are not alone.
May their sweet potatoes go down easy.
May they get cards or a phone call. Amen.

P.S. Mary, if you know of a saint
who is also a techie (e.g.,
Saint Isidore of Seville, patron saint
of the Internet and computers), please
ask him to show the nurses how to Zoom
so mothers can see their kids and grandkids.
The Atlantic says children born this spring
will be dubbed Generation C and grow
into Baby Zoomers, Coronials,
or Quaranteens. Their parents will follow
quarantrends then guzzle quarantinis
finalizing their covidivorces.
Mary, it's May, the month we crown you
with lilacs and lilies. This poem's for you.

The Bentley, a glitzy hotel lacking
customers, opened up to the homeless
and fed them Domino's as a midnight
snack. Was this your work, Mary? The Upper
East Side rooms have views of the 59th
Street Bridge, premium bedding, and cable.
I don't know how New Yorkers keep the faith.
They remind me of one big epic poem
compressed beyond belief into a single
sonnet. Or they're like a school of clownfish
trapped in the gut of a whale. When their time
is almost up, they simply keep swimming.
May each New Yorker emerge like Jonah—
the moral of the story, resilience.

The moral of the story is: hoarders
aren't crazy, after all. Or: Wyoming's
a great place to keep living. Or: Why not
invest in baby chicks? Everyone could
use an omelet once in a while. When this
is over, let's run back into the sea
and float, looking up at the moon and stars.
I've always been afraid to swim at night
but now that I've faced so many fears, this
one seems small, inconsequential. Lifeguards
are usually on their phones anyway
texting their friends or checking Facebook.
When everything is back to normal, let's
spend our money on whatever we want.

Surgery girls pool their money for wings
while the Tyson plant remains closed
and Broadway's Saint Christopher
helps baby loggerheads cross the Hudson.
Remember Dolittle's Pushmi-Pullyu—
one half Colorado's gay governor,
the other, Florida's straight governor?
Our kids outgrow their childhoods
while our president loves profit and doo-wopping.
We've had so many deaths in our fifty states
we're on our knees, saying the rosary.
Mary, do you know the saints who stayed
at the Bentley last night and lacked nothing?
P.S. There is no moral to this story.

Blues Clues (an Excerpt)

4.24.20

Remember the B-52s' "Private Idaho?" Living "underground like a wild potato / don't go on the patio..." I hope your daughter is underground, under her covers sleeping, and that these hives are indeed strawberry hives. My mother is nauseous this morning, another symptom identified with Covid-19. There are 47 positive cases in the nursing home now, with 5 deaths. Sixteen workers also tested positive. There are only 80 patients total—my mother's testing negative so far, though the math is not in her favor. My friend Kathy Lawrence wrote a piece about her Aunt Maggie lost to the Pandemic of 1918, in Astoria, Queens, when it was at its peak just like the coronavirus is now these 102 years later. Maggie's parents had survived the Irish potato famine as children, but Maggie moved to New York at just the wrong time. It's the wrong time for my mother to be where she is. It's the wrong time of year to be stuck inside. I miss swimming in the pool at the condo, which is closed even though the CDC says "chlorine and bromine...should inactivate the virus in the water." What do you think the B-52s meant by "beware of the pool / blue bottomless pool"?

4.25.20

When the B-52s said, *Beware of the pool / blue bottomless pool,*
I was a mom with two little kids and a man who flew away
down some *dirty back road* to his own *private Idaho* where he was
runnin' around and *53 miles west of Venus. Give me back my man,*
I said to the *quiche Lorraine* who stole him, or I will *party out of*
bounds with a *devil in my car*. And I did. My roaring thirties. Ha.
I think they meant beware of something beautiful on the surface
that might suck you under if you don't know how to swim. A riptide.
A politician. (That was fun.) A virus. *Hoo hoo hoo hoo hoo hoo…*
I always come back to Covid. A friend waving to her mother
through a nursing home window. A daughter covered in hives.
This wild planet. Yesterday we walked in the rain with our invincible
umbrellas. Today there's sun. What if we write our own "Song
for a Future Generation"? For my grandson and your grandnephews,
all these lovely little boys in our life.

4.25.20

Yes, let's! This morning I read a gorgeous poem "Letter to My Great, Great Grandchild" by J. P. Grasser, which was the Poem-a-Day from Poets.org. The poem begins: *Oh button, don't go thinking we loved pianos more than elephants, air conditioning more than air.* I felt the pang of guilt that has become cliché—what kind of a world are we leaving for them? That was also the impetus for Grasser, but his poem transcends all that and his process statement concludes that "protecting the future demands presence." So here goes. "Song for a Future Generation." What will you invent, our darling boys who will one day be men? What will you see that we could not? Who will you love? Who will love you back? Will you sew, knit, bake a cake from scratch? Will you travel to Antarctica just for the hell of it? Will you write a poem remembering us when we're gone? We wish you wild laughter and kindhearted pranks, puns, bike wheelies, guitars that remind you of your dads… (Maureen, take it from here!)

4.26.20

Wanna be the ruler of the galaxy? Wanna be the king
of the universe? Today you're riding your scooter six feet
from the girl next door who is named Arizona,
whose parents are rocket scientists. You miss your friend
Miles, though, so I wish you unlimited hours with future friends.
I know you will be an entertainer because you have exquisite
timing. Will you sing or breakdance or tell stories with your body
the way you do now? And will you build the first LEGO city to welcome
everybody who wants to live there, no matter what, no matter who?
For you are Galaxy Boy, you are the King of Hearts. We have
left you so little to work with, my love, but it is yours
and your hands are amazing. Please remember this when
you miss me and a pandemic barrels down Route 25.

in memory of George Floyd (October 14, 1973–May 25, 2020)

Here is your image
in our DNA, Oh Son—
here your own last prayer.

At eight, you wrote you'd grow up
to be a Supreme Court Justice.

What We Write about When We Don't Write about the Pandemic

with illustrations by Chloe Koons

Last night there was so much rain and wind, I had trouble sleeping. Hurricane season officially begins two weeks from today, but weather patterns are changing. I kept waking up and checking where the floor meets my sliders. Sure enough, at 4 p.m., a puddle the size of a saucer. I wiped up the water, too upset to go back to sleep. Then I watched the finale of *How to Get Away With Murder*, which I'd taped. I love Viola Davis, who is from RI like I am. Her character Annalise had bigger problems than I do. I finally went to bed, thinking I should have taken a picture of the rainwater as evidence—but there would be no trial, only a wet towel. When I had the new windows installed last year, Scott said, "I guarantee they won't break if they're hit by a coconut. Hurricane glass will crack, but never shatter." When I asked about water intrusion, he said, "No one can promise you that. And if they do, they're lying."

*

It's so weird to not be personally worrying about hurricane season. Colorado's as far from the Atlantic as I've ever been. It's not like we don't flood here or burst into flames or get buried in snow, and there's this strange pollution thing over the mountains—what is that?—and once in a while a little wind. Anyway, I've been unpacking boxes from Florida and here's something I found in an old journal, ca. 2005 (big hurricane season): *I swear I love snakes, but my neighbor is afraid of the twenty-foot pythons in the Everglades. He is a drunk, but he is not a liar. He says they will soon rule the world.*

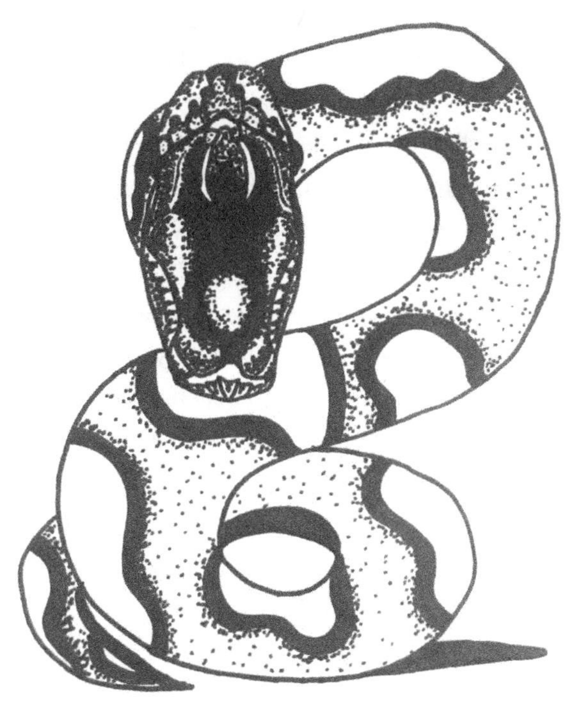

This past fall a student told me about a python coming out of someone's Florida toilet and biting him! I must have black-boxed it, shut the lid on it, so to speak. It sounds like a story from the *National Enquirer*, but also a story that feeds into my fears. When I Google it now, it is not only true, but it's happened more than once! In May of 2019, a Coral Springs man lifted the seat and a four-foot snake bit him on the arm. In Australia, a woman was bitten on her behind in the middle of the night. Imagine? It's happening all over the world—North Carolina, Thailand, India, England, and New York City (from a toilet in an apartment on the 19th floor.) Tamer El-Ghobashy of the *Wall Street Journal* explained, "Snakes are good swimmers who can hold their breath for a long time, and are well capable of swimming upward and squeezing through tight spaces if needed."

The only four-syllable word I could find that rhymes with snake is *radiopaque*, the term for any material that inhibits the passage of X-rays and gamma rays. One example of a radiopaque substance would be human bone, which appears white or gray on an X-ray, although the last time I went for an X-ray, my bones were neither white nor gray but teal blue, the color that best complements my hair, which is a light copper chestnut. You might also come across the word radiopaque at your local airport security if, for example, you wrapped your egg salad sandwich in aluminum foil (radiopaque) instead of plastic wrap (radiolucent). Personally, I think the word radiopaque should be spelled radio-opaque, since its opposite is radiolucent. See what I mean? I'd like to know who makes up these words. The next time I go for X-rays I might be wearing my new wig, "Rubies at Night." Then we'll see what color my bones are.

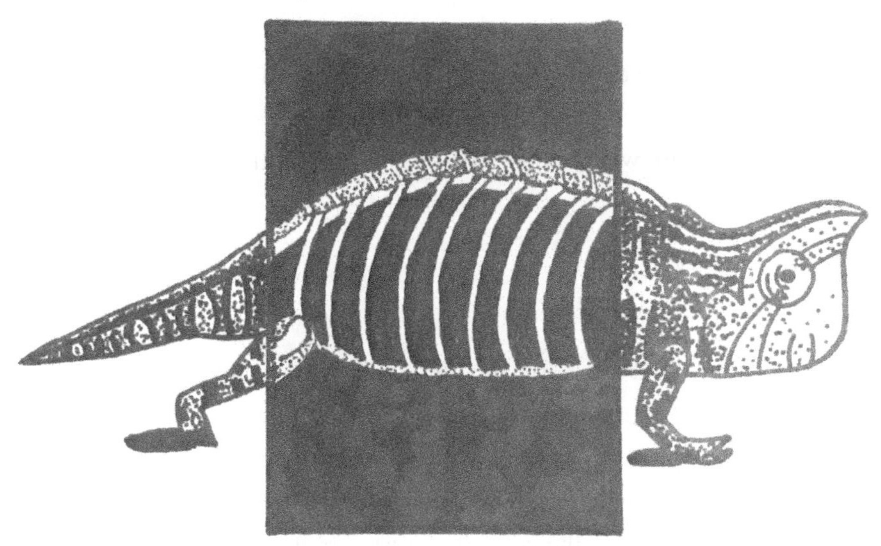

Radiopaque sounds like a rave band opening up for Praga Khan, Blümchen, or Glostik. I don't know really what any of these bands sound like, but I remember when a student referenced Glostik in a poem and I was quite sure (though I was wrong!) that she was writing about those glow-in-the-dark necklaces people used to sell from kiosks on the boardwalk. I was sure her use of Glostik's sound was an interesting example of synesthesia. The next year a student referenced the band Sublime and I asked—Why is this capitalized? Why isn't this an image instead? I couldn't use my senses to hear Sublime the way the rest of the class could. This morning I am reading that chameleon bones glow an eerie blue under ultraviolet light. Our human bones might glow too, but our skin and muscles cover them up. Chameleon bones don't change color. It's just that bony outgrowths along their skeletons sit just beneath the skin, which is thin enough for the glow to shine through. Under that same UV light, scorpions glow bright green.

The only time I ever saw a scorpion I was walking down Surf Road not a mile from home. It was a major moment for me, as I'd been wondering my entire life what it would be like to come face to face with a real scorpion. I felt the same way about sharks, tidal waves, rabies, lockjaw, polio, rapists, volcanoes, and quicksand: things every American girl should be on the lookout for. I love that chameleon bones don't change color under UV light and that scorpions glow green. I love the name Glostik for a band. This morning I sat up in bed and didn't fear a goddam thing.

In *Parasite*, my favorite movie of 2019, several times the character Ki-woo says, "This is so metaphorical." Today everything seems like a metaphor. The woman in Maryland who found a live scorpion in her bag of spinach from a Giant grocery store. Poop in the pork because the conveyor belt at the meat-packing plant was going too fast. Is my love of bacon finally coming to an end? What about my spinach-and-bacon salads? Martha Stewart says to make a hot dressing with the bacon to delightfully wilt the spinach on contact.

*

When I first started teaching poetry writing, it was to a handful of visual artists who were a lot like kids, kids on a brave mission, as none in the group had ever written a poem. So I found Kenneth Koch (a Pisces), used his book, *Wishes, Lies, and Dreams, Teaching Children to Write Poetry*, and started their experience with metaphors, which Koch simply calls *comparisons*. Here is my (a Libra's) current favorite metaphor: "He's mean as a motherfucker. He's Satan with a heart." (my partner, Lori Anderson, a Leo). P.S. If anyone is wondering why the zodiac showed up in this short segment of "What We Write about When We Don't Write about the Pandemic," I don't blame you. I was wondering that myself.

I wish I knew a little more about the zodiac! I was talking to my niece Athena today. She is 27, living in Texas, and is unsure what to do next in her life—nurse, teacher, social worker, lawyer. I told her that her Saturn was returning and a big change was coming. When we hung up I Googled around to send her some websites. And, lo and behold, my second Saturn Return is happening right now—between March and December of 2020. How lucky am I to live to have a second chance at something transformative, although I know Saturn Returning can also mean loss and death. Do you know any good Zoom astrologists?

How about Luke Dani Blue at Seagoat Astrology? They're giving free pandemic readings and I bet they would love to take a look at the chart of someone in her second Saturn Return. Awesome and terrifying at the same time! My first Saturn returned to smash a marriage to bits then give me a really cool life without gin. My second Saturn Return began with Hurricane Wilma and progressed through a couple of years you may remember as deadly or death-defying, depending on poetic point of view. Now Sebby has burst into my room with his newly constructed LEGO Minecraft Zombie Cave. He's LEGO-shooting at a zombie and shouting *Mwa ha ha*—just like a real villain.

❋

When he was six, Ben used to love to take me to jail. I'd ask for my lawyer and he'd say, *Wait in here*, putting me in his bedroom and shutting the door. I'd hear him ask his brothers and cousins if they wanted to be my lawyer, but mostly they ignored him. Ben was the oldest of the bunch and didn't know what a lawyer was. The other little kids didn't either. Once in a while a toddler would take pity on me and say, *I'll be the lawyer*, and take my big hand in his little hand and lead me out of the room. *But she broke the law!* Ben would say. *She broke the law!* Ben is nine now, still obsessed with fairness. I will be 59 next month. When my first Saturn returned, I sued my New York City slumlord and won. I used the money to pay off my student loans. I felt like the winner in a game show. Now I feel like it's all a game. Now I have so much to lose.

❄

Things I stand to lose: owls, real and fake; the color turquoise (is this a lesbian color? I heard it is!); an entire set of Le Pens; fish tacos with mango; mango mango mango; the drive down 25 to Albuquerque; crying when I cross the border into New Mexico; feeling enchanted; juniper, prickly pear, roadrunners, Sandias; the drive up 25 to Boulder; stopping at the park by the Safeway in Trinidad to walk my dog; my dog; the Sangre de Cristos, the Rockies, the Flatirons; snow (angels), heavy snow, light snow; lots of snow; aspens, catalpas, lilacs; McIntosh Lake, eagles, Longs Peak, Twin Sisters; white pelicans in Colorado (migrating); brown pelicans in Florida (enjoying the sea); Miami; mango; the sea. The sea.

§

Howl

for America, after Ginsberg

America! I'm with you in "Allergy Valley" (PA)
where my husband locks me out of the apartment and I'm so angry I throw
a lawn chair at the door
I'm with you in Aurora (CO)
where my oncologist and I go outside to view the eclipse
I'm with you in the Bronx
where I get into trouble performing a poem about racism and the patriarchy
I'm with you in the Berkshires
where I step out of a movie theater to see a bear and her cub on the sidewalk
I'm with you in Cleveland
where Tamir holds a toy gun and is killed with a real one
I'm with you in Croton-on-Hudson
where I find Hansberry's grave in the pouring rain
I'm with you in Dollywood
where I have my picture taken with Dolly's cousin who looks just like
I imagine Dolly would if she hadn't had plastic surgery
I'm with you in Denny's
where Julie and I contemplate ordering from the "baconalia" menu (e.g.
a caramel sundae topped with bacon)
I'm with you on the East Side (Lower)
where I sleep in a loft bed with a desk and typewriter underneath,
and wake to shower in a stall in the kitchen

I'm with you on Eubank Blvd. (ABQ)
    where six lanes of traffic come to a complete stop for a scared Chihuahua
I'm with you on Fullerton (CHI)
    where Our Lady of the Underpass appears below I-90 and Tanya Saracho
    writes a play about her
I'm with you in Flint
    where toxic water flows from the faucet
I'm with you in the Grand Hyatt Hotel (NYC)
    where Richard McDonald is served the ceremonial 50 billionth McDonald's
    hamburger in 1984
I'm with you in Greenwich Village (NYC)
    where I buy my first vibrator at the Pink Pussycat Boutique
I'm with you in Harvey
    where a hawk seeks refuge in William Bruso's cab and nine trillion gallons
    of rain fall on Houston
I'm with you in Harvey
    where a fangtooth snake eel with tiny decomposed eyes washes up on a beach
    in Texas City
I'm with you in Irma
    where I spy you with my enormous eye (September 6, 2017)
I'm with you in Irma
    where I evacuate with John and Cindy, where we wait in gas lines one hundred
    cars long, where we are not sure we'll have homes to which we can return
    (September 9, 2017)
I'm with you in Jensen Beach (FL)
    where I find a dead baby loggerhead and bury it deep in the sand
I'm with you in Jersey
    where Ginsberg is born and so am I

I'm with you in Kansas City (both Kansas and Missouri)
    where I break my vegetarian diet with BBQ twice
I'm with you in Kivalina (AK)
    where the city is melting
I'm with you in LA
    where I eat a fig off a tree
I'm with you in Lincoln Square (CHI)
    where Cobalt gives me my first tattoo and hers: a three-hour sunflower
I'm with you in Mingo Park (OH)
    where I listen to Prince on my iPod
I'm with you in Memphis
    where Martin Luther King is shot at the Lorraine Motel as ducks roam the lobby of the Peabody
I'm with you in Nebraska
    where Malcolm X is born, and where the largest porch swing in the world holds twenty-five Nebraskans
I'm with you in Newport
    where tourists visit the mansions and Cliff Walk
I'm with you in Oklahoma
    where the earth is red
I'm with you in Orange County
    where all good Republicans go to die—or so thinks Ronald Reagan
I'm with you in the Panhandle
    where meth labs flourish and sometimes explode
I'm with you in Providence
    where I buy medical marijuana for my mother
I'm with you in Quest Diagnostics
    where I get my blood work done year after year

I'm with you in Queens

where I write this line: "Only Olive owned ostentatious orgasms;

the puerile position of pomp belonged to Popeye."

I'm with you in Riverdale

where I live in a studio with my daughter and my lover builds a loft for her

and we all feel rich

I'm with you in Revere Beach (MA)

where my boyfriend tells me he is gay and I try to convince him he's not

I'm with you in Seattle

where I ride the Great Wheel with Jay and Kristine

I'm with you in St. Louis

where my sister leaves their Christianity for her own

I'm with you in Tucson

where I learn to make sun tea

I'm with you in TGI Fridays

where my Cobb salad is so huge my friend from England is sure it is for the

whole table to share

I'm with you in Utah

where I contemplate a leap from the Tower of Babel

I'm with you in Uxbridge (MA)

where, at Southwick's Zoo, my sister is accosted by a goat who puts his

hooves on her tiny shoulders when she freezes, afraid to feed him a paper cup

of goat food

I'm with you in Venice (FL)

where the sand is black from crushed bones of the Pleistocene

I'm with you in Venice (CA)

where Tom gets sober and rides across country on his putt putt motorcycle

and we fly down the West Side Highway at midnight

I'm with you in Woonsocket (RI)
    where I spend a summer working in the Coby Glass factory making Christmas ornaments
I'm with you in Wrigleyville
    where I watch a Cubs game from a beloved poet's porch
I'm with you in the XXX movie theater the Roxy
    where my friend sells tickets, where I only go as far as the lobby to return the sweater I borrowed
I'm with you in *Xanadu* (the American movie)
    where we eat popcorn as Olivia Newton-John transforms into an '80s Terpsichore, one of the nine Muses, on roller skates
I'm with you in Yellowstone
    where bear where moose where wolverine and lynx
I'm with you in Youngstown
    where, in a hotel halfway between Chicago and New York, we hear the Rodney King verdict and cry ourselves to sleep
I'm with you in Zion National Park
    where the name, Mukuntuweap, is changed in 1918 because the NPS thinks visitors won't visit the park if they can't pronounce it
I'm with you in the Zuni Pueblo (NM)
    where the world is divided into six directions: north, west, south, east, above, and below

Death Is Not a Riddle

Aunt Ruth, Aunt Pearl, Aunt Fran, and Aunt Terri, gone
the way of extinct apples—Maiden's Blush and Prairie Spy

The Notorious B.I.G., the Big Bopper, Ernest Borgnine, Bruce Lee,
Brandon Lee, Bette Davis, Betty Berzon, Betty Shabazz, and Bashō

Coco Chanel, who may have been a Nazi spy; Celia Cruz; Caucasus moose;
Carolina parakeet and Cuban macaw (all wiped out)

Doomed Deadheads: one died in a car accident; one was murdered and dumped
in a ditch; seven are still missing, their whereabouts unknown

Emily Brontë, Emily Dickinson, Emily Post (born as Emily Price), Elizabeth Peña,
Dead Earth Zombies, the Egyptian Book of the Dead

Four and twenty blackbirds, Four Horsemen of the Apocalypse, Redd Foxx,
and the Four-Dead-in-Five-Seconds-Gunfight (El Paso, 1881)

Grover Cleveland, Greta Garbo, Günter Grass, and my beloved Grammy,
Graham Greene, George Michael, and Gabriel García Márquez

Heraclitus, devoured by dogs; Henry Thomas, combusted spontaneously in an
easy chair; Horace Hunley, sunk in a submarine of his own invention

Imogene Coca from Alzheimer's; Ike Turner from an overdose; Ingrid Bergman
from breast cancer; Isadora Duncan, strangulation by her own scarf

John Paul I (conspiracy), John D. Rockefeller III (car crash), John Doe (California):
Death is not a riddle, yet we are often stumped. (1978)

Kali, of Hindu goddess fame, wearing a necklace of human heads;
Katharine Hepburn (tumor); Karen Carpenter (anorexia, 91 pounds at the end)

Lucille Clifton and Langston Hughes, dead of poetry; Leon Russell and Leonard Cohen,
dead of song; Lou Reed, Liberace, and Luther Vandross, dead of love

Muriel Rukeyser (whose "The Book of The Dead" riffs on the Egyptian);
Marianne Moore; Henri Michaux; Czeslaw Milosz; and Michelangelo

Nixon, Marni: the "ghost soprano," whose singing replaced Audrey Hepburn's in *My
Fair Lady*; Natalie Wood's in *West Side Story*; Deborah Kerr's in *The King and I*

Odetta and Tillie Olsen: opalescent feminists; and O, all those O's—Georgia O'Keeffe,
Carroll O'Connor (*All in the Family*) and Maureen O'Sullivan (Tarzan's gal)

Professor Marvel, aka Wizard of Oz, eternal on page and screen; Prince Rogers Nelson,
previously known as [symbol], and Freddie Prinze, really and sincerely dead

Queens—e.g., Victoria, Isabella, Mary, Elizabeth I, Nefertiti, Cleopatra, Catherine, Marie-Antoinette; Karen Ann Quinlan (and her "right to die" case)

Ride, Sally: first American woman in space, youngest American astronaut in space, first known LGBT astronaut. See also: Rutkiewicz, Wanda: first woman to summit K2

Superman (Doomsday), Sam Shepard (Lou Gehrig's), Soupy Sales and Carl Sagan (both cancer), Selena (murdered), Shel Silverstein and Margaret Sanger (both heart)

Tupac Shakur, Thalo Kersey, and T. Thumb—*[W]hose Life and adventures containe[d] many strange and wonderfull accidents*

Uncle Miltie (Milton Berle) as well as my own Uncle Will, Uncle Ray, Uncle Edgar, and Uncle Noel; John Updike ("Tall and beaky-looking" reads his obit)

Vivian Vance, Sid Vicious, Kurt Vonnegut, Vincent van Gogh, and the Virgin Mary: some died vague, some vast, of voice, of vodka, very far away

Walt Whitman, Whitney Houston, Phillis Wheatley, William Wordsworth, Wang Wei, Barry White, and Oscar Wilde: all of whom knew how to sing

Malcolm X, Madame X, Professor X, Innocent X, Leo X, Clement X, and Xerxes
X is *a ladder of swords that only the shaman can climb in bare feet*

Young—Loretta (*The Farmer's Daughter*), Coleman (first Black mayor of Detroit), Alan (Wilbur Post, owner of Mr. Ed), and Brigham (who led the Mormon migration)

Zappa, Zsa Zsa, Zillah, Zapata, Ziyang, Zanuck, Zanuck, Zimbalist, Zelda, Zora, Zane

Z End

Resurrection Sonnets

"It's not really death if you can return."
John Steppling

My father comes back as a red cardinal.
And my freckled friend, in her last poem,
offers to haunt me after her so-called
untimely death. Why not, I say. Zombies
are scary, but my friend will be more
like Casper. Remember that "friendly ghost"?
Now my mother comes back as a suicide
bomber, complete with trigger and child
welfare services tracking her every move.
My dream book says I am trying to kill
any chance of a long life, choosing
whatever boasts a skull and crossbones—
my bandana, my necklace. My ring tone:
Blue Oyster Cult's "Don't Fear the Reaper."

I spy the Reaper once as I turn blue
from lack of O2. He scythes everything,
including my jeans which he tears at the knee.
A nurse stabs an EpiPen in my thigh,
and I come back as Banksy's flower bomber
in Jerusalem or Amarillo, my
first stop Publix where I buy carnations
and Mylar balloons to chuck at harassers
who come back as an entire rainforest.
Dream book says: Death in the Afternoon
is trying to make me see I am both
bull and matador, hoof and cape, *olé!*
Drink three to five of these slowly, it bubbles
and soothes. By nightfall I come back to life.

Nightfall I come back to life—so soothing
the vampire's kiss seconds before the fangs
sink silky with their myth of immortal life.
Now my cat comes back as a poet, prickly
pear jelly on her toast. See that bicyclist
over there? He was once my caged hamster.
And here is my great-grandmother, her re-
fashioned face the face of a manatee.
What about the extinct passenger pigeon?
Can she come back as herself, her species
surviving, after all, to upstage texting? *Men*
feign themselves dead and endure mock funerals.
A new Emerson peeks through the blinds—
all the honking below, God in the exhaust.

It's exhausting to believe in God.
So many hard-won death scenarios.
Andrea Dworkin says God is the ultimate
pornographer—our suffering turns him on.
But I think he's a fractal, an evolving
symmetry, and death is impossible,
like squaring a circle. Irrational
numbers like pi promise eternity.
Complex numbers with a zero can be
purely imaginary, like heaven.
I wish I'd learned to play the harp, the angel
sleeves on my gauzy white dress inspiring
politicians to come back as super-
humble heroes and/or Justice Leaguers.

Some beleaguered heroes humbly seek justice
in the afterlife. But what if heaven's a scam?
Or what if it's *half-finished* and it's our
job to lay the joists and lift the drywall?
The man who installed my kitchen backsplash
died of a heart attack before I could hire
him to fix my soggy walls after Irma.
I wonder if he'll come back to Florida
as a green (his favorite color) parrot
or a Bismarck palm at TreeWorld Wholesale.
He'd better hurry if he plans to make
landfall in our sorrowful sinking state.
Miami, built on landfill, now in hospice,
hears the red dirge of American songbirds.

Yes, And

When you bury your grandmother, you assume that's the last you'll see of her. But after Katrina, a man found his granny's remains in the soggy cemetery, her coffin dug up by the storm surge.

Yes, and there is a name for the kind of grief that rises after a storm, but I have lost that too in the moon-faced flood.

Yes, and there is that fatigue—the funeral/hurricane preparations over—the emergency supplies gone, only the sad heart left.

Yes, and did you know the heart of the country lies in Kansas? Or South Dakota? If you add Puerto Rico, which is legally a territory, so you can't really add it, but I can and will, the heart would move a little to the left of Iowa—I'm not a cardiologist— weeping.

Yes, and in the Keys, house debris is piled two stories high with fridges, couches, and tables sticking out like a hideous sculpture. My colleague goes with his church on weekends to help, the slow slog of getting back to normal after Hurricane Irma.

Yes, and Ballast Key [24°31′26″N 81°57′51″W] was once the southernmost point in the contiguous states continuously above water. (*You put water into a bottle it becomes the bottle*, Bruce Lee.)

Yes, and I made my own sandbags when Kmart and Home Depot were sold out. I took the plastic pail and shovel I'd bought for the kids to the beach and filled up the legs of a pair of tights then cut out the crotch and knotted the top. Voila! Two sandbags. Not that they did much good.

Yes, and on the island of Barbuda the water became the island. So we drove into the mountains and the water became the mountains. The glaciers at 14,000 feet became the water and the light became the water too.

Yes, and my husband and I went on an Alaskan cruise, a failed attempt to save our marriage. We heard the glaciers crackle and then saw a chunk plunge into the sea. I thought it a sad metaphor for us since he melted away two months later. Of course, it's not a metaphor at all.

Yes, and metaphors are only as effective as the things they compare. Alaska was on my bucket list until I started to die for real, then I thought: Alaska is Florida and Florida is Colorado, and Colorado is Illinois, but nothing is New York but New York.

Yes, and since I had to empty all my closets for the water restoration company, I have two buckets in the living room—a blue one holding Bob's fishing pole and a white one holding a couple of mops. Buckets seem a strange metaphor for death, right?

Yes, and now the first snowstorm of the season (Aiden with an "e", not *Desperately Seeking Susan*'s Aidan with an "a") follows the jet stream south over the peaks and dumps buckets on the butterflies and the bees. [40.1672° N, 105.1019° W]

Yes, and here in Florida we have the first green flag from the lifeguard hut since Irma. It's safe to go in the water again, which is a lot closer than it used to be, so much erosion. My neighbor warned that the first step is like a Slip 'N Slide, a deep decline, then plop—the water was up to his waist.

Yes, and here in Colorado it's back to 70° this week. Wingless snow angels, dripping roofs. I used to admire the hell out of weather, the one thing science couldn't predict past 48 hours. I wonder if that's still true.

Yes, and when we evacuated we intended to go to Naples but then Irma headed west so we went to Tampa but could only stay for one night, as Tampa was being evacuated too. All the hotels in Atlanta were sold out by then, so we wound up in the Panhandle, a tiny patch of Florida that was spared.

Yes, and I stood watch on the shore of Colorado as my country drowned to the south and burned to the north. Stocks rose to the east and in the west there was more death in ten minutes than I could fathom. The cancer inside me longed to live. It wound around my spine like morning glories.

Yes, and my sister has started the tradition of bringing her grandchildren to the cemetery. Yesterday when she bought a sweatshirt for "dad," meaning her son-in-law, little Nick thought she meant *her* dad, his great-grandfather who died before he was born. He asked, "But is this sweatshirt big enough to fit over his wings?"

Yes, and the Day of the Dead celebration begins this Friday—three weeks of *gigantes* and sugar skulls and altars for the ancestors. It's always been my favorite holiday, but especially now, in the middle of all this dear life.

27 Lines about Death

1. My father and my cat died the same year. They both had black hair.

2. I'm not sure I've adequately mourned my father, as he died when I was a mess, going through a divorce.

3. My grandfather died the same year they closed Newark Airport because three planes crashed in Elizabeth, which had nothing and everything to do with flying.

4. I could never be sure if the kids at the Children's Hospital, where I spent fourth grade, went home or died, but a certain child would sometimes be gone by lunch and the nurses wouldn't tell us anything.

5. After my brother crashed his race car, he said he wouldn't mind dying behind the wheel.

6. After my sister crashed her car, she was in a coma. To this day she doesn't remember a thing about it.

7. The tenth-most-dangerous activity is heli-skiing. First you jump out of a helicopter, then you ski down a mountain, then you parachute to the ground. (No comment.)

8. And what about orgasms, *la petite mort*? It's important to have as many as possible (especially for women) in preparation for death.

9. I can't remember the last time I thought about death during orgasm, although I was worried my dead grandparents were watching me the first time.

10. I once saw a child-ghost at an artists' colony and a painter said a prayer to help her to the other side.

11. I yelled at a prankster ghost once to leave my daughter alone when she lived at the Ansonia.

12. I used sage and a gentle tone to get rid of the ghost in Lewisburg who was fond of turning on the lights in the middle of the night.

13. I guess ghosts aren't really dead, are they? Departed, gone, no more, passed on, asleep, at peace, exanimate?

14. Depending on what psychic you listen to, dead people might not even be fully dead. It sounds exhausting now that I think about it.

15. I'm laughing the laugh of the dead right now. All around me: clacking teeth and skulls thrown back.

16. My favorite death movie is the Pixar animated *Coco*—so many skulls!—and I am not alone. It has a 97% rating on Rotten Tomatoes.

17. My favorite death movie is *Harold and Maude*. I love when Harold gives Maude a present and she promptly throws it in the lake.

18. My favorite death poem? Who can say! So many to choose from.

19. For a lot of poets, the term "death poem" might be an oxymoron. Or do I mean redundant? I like the words *elegy* and *elegiac*.

20. It sounds as though a jay could fly right out of *elegiac* even though I know it's usually doves released at fancy funerals. It's possible I saw that gesture in a movie about death.

21. And crows, of course. I saw a murder of them yesterday and thought, damn, I can't even put these guys in a death poem anymore because a publisher said they're being overused. (Do I care?)

22. It's been three full weeks since I wrote a line about death. Suddenly I miss it.

23. Sometimes I miss the living as much as I do the dead.

24. If I can text you from the afterlife—if I have a phone and a signal—I promise I will!

25. Now that this is about to end it feels more like a bucket list. Or, as my friend Linda prefers to say, a fuck-it list.

26. I was thinking of calling mine a basket list, as my wish is to get in a hot-air balloon before I die.

27. At 104, Pulitzer Prize winner Herman Wouk headed the DeathList 2019—fifty celebrities chosen for their likelihood to die in that year. He made it to May, then died in his sleep.

§

Floridada: Our 51st State

Whereas, the new proposed state of South
Florida may float off into the Caribbean
if we wait for Rick Scott, we propose
a divorce. Tallahassee never loved
Okeechobee anyway, and the scary
hurricane thing, well, who needs that?
Whereas, the Turkey Point nuclear reactors
are well past their prime, we insist
on palimony, as we've shipped a lot of loot
north and it's never come back—and our ship
was very dear to us. Tallahassee knows
that! We promised ourselves we wouldn't cry
for 150 years (our ultimate submersion),
but the mangroves are threatening to walk
and the pigeon plums are packing their trunks.
Whereas, the Everglades are on fire
and ghost orchids are hitching rides and
thousands of tree islands stand on tippy toes,
we draw the line at Brevard, Orange, Polk,
Hillsborough, and Pinellas. Above that,
there are pelicans to relocate and several feet
of seawater to bail before century's end.
Whereas, our buckets are the plastic kind

we give to our kiddies, we request
a split (not spit), a schism (not prison), and a
big old raft of miracles to save our soggy asses.

Stairway to Heaven Sonnet

Florida's state bird is the crane, by which we mean
green, orange, and yellow construction cranes that hang
a mile or more above us on the beach and swing their pointy
arms all around like slo-mo highwire ballerinas.
They stand while they sleep and each weekday morning
call out their metal duets then begin their pointe work.
I ask my love: do you think that crane would crush
us in our bed like palmetto bugs if it fell north?
Of course it would, my amour says and that night
wakes up screaming, flapping very human arms.
Sometimes we feel watched over as we grab our
water wings and float like the dead on top of the sea.
Sometimes our necks ache from craning at the cranes
that sway to Led Zeppelin at dawn, all flute and wonder.

Florida Doll Sonnet

I love Fresh Market but always feel underdressed
squeezing overpriced limes. Louis Vuitton,
Gucci, Fiorucci, and all the ancient East Coast girls
with their scarecrow limbs and Joker grins.
Their silver fox husbands, rosy from tanning beds,
steady their ladies who shuffle along in Miu Miu's
(not muumuus) and make me hide behind towers
of handmade soaps and white pistachios. Who
knew I'd still feel like the high school fat girl
some thirty-odd years later? My Birkenstocks
and my propensity for Fig Newtons? Still, whenever
I'm face to face with a face that is no more real
than a doll's, I try to love my crinkles, my saggy
chin skin. My body organic, with no preservatives.

Anti(dis)establishmentarianism Sonnet

When Key West passed its symbolic resolution
in support of same-sex marriage in 2004, I knew
what was next. My lover would want a minister,
a cake, the whole shebang. I was a happy outcast
from the legal noise and noose of wedlock. I thought
I was safe as long as I lived in Florida, state of
restrictive laws: no women allowed to parachute
on Sunday; no men allowed in strapless gowns.
Once upon a time, I was felonious and free as a
pelican brigade, I was endangered as a ghost orchid.
But now I'm registered at Bed Bath & Beyond,
fussing over a seating chart. What is marriage,
you say, if not for the brave, and what is love if not
for all? Please pass me the gown and the parachute.

If Not Joy

1

When it's 55 degrees in Florida
it's time to take out the Uggs. The tile
on the apartment floor is icy and my heat
is basically like a hair dryer turned on low.
But I digress—weather is such a First World/
boring topic. What I wanted to tell you is
that after all these years of thinking
all life forms need phosphorus, scientists
have found "life" made from arsenic instead.
There's such a microorganism in California's
Mono Lake, which looks like another planet—
speaking of which, we have to rethink
life in the cosmos, right? I had mono
as a teenager and slept for a week straight
but never dreamt of arsenic. What is life
if not carbon? What is weather
if not sun or rain? What is writing
if not free association?

2

I love that you started in Florida
with a digression, Denise, then spiraled
until you landed in that arsenic-laced
lake called Mono, saltier than the beloved
sea we both dodge in December while tourists
paddle around as if they have feathers
and gulls' feet and could never get frostbite
in a million years. (Or seven days.) Twenty
thousand creationists met Sunday near
Boulder, where I now sit wrapped in wool
and writing to you from a real winter.
Those zany literalists. Those disembodied
Darwin debunkers. We don't have to rethink
anything, as it turns out, but today I drove
straight into the Rockies to see if I've evolved
past my reptilian fear of black ice and
avalanches and angry God people. Just
me, the snow, the mountains.

3

On my way to Ohio in just a few minutes!
But before I go I have to tell you about the naturalist
who led my recent adventure to the Galápagos.
He was asked the question—has anyone
come on this trip with religious conviction
that Darwin was wrong? *Oh yes,* he replied.
When pressed he said he negotiated the question
straight up. *I get it, I'm from Ecuador,*
a Catholic country, but I'm a scientist
and religion is a nice fairy tale. I was shocked
that he didn't try to make us feel any better
about death or divine purpose, but relieved too.
I hate those willy-nilly types that say
religion and science complement each other,
even though on some days I am that
willy-nilly myself. I love that you are
in the mountains. I am at sea level
about to rise in the air on Southwest.

4

I never had mono, but I sure tried hard
to get it my freshman year in college (Catholic),
and all those boys I kissed were fervent
evolutionists (revolutionists). (It was the sixties.)
Now Francis agrees with his former popes
that evolution and creation go hand in hand. Okay.
That God is not a magician. What?
Just look at those giant tortoises. That
photo of you smiling beside one proves
both Darwin and some crazy cat somewhere
possessed wild imaginations. (Magic wands.)
Not to mention the blue-footed booby!
And the red-footed one! And the two of us
colliding over the Hudson, bursting with words,
so long ago we must be ancient by now.
How did it feel to inhabit the same air
as an ancient tortoise on a mythical island?
Thank you, Denise, for the word: *archipelago.*

5

I believe I caught mono from taking a sip
from a water bottle, not from a boy's lips.
I called in sick for the first time in my life, thinking
I had a cold or a hangover then fell asleep
and when I woke up it was a different month.
Did you hear about these new flu strains
resistant to antibiotics? Doctors are blaming
the people of India who give their infants
antibiotics because of the poor sanitation.
Well, doctors are really blaming the dirty
drinking water, the germs that live on
even after they have been boiled. It is hard
to think about being on life's spectrum,
our life and death no big deal in the long run.
That is what it felt like on the Galápagos,
the sea and wind blasting, the volcanoes
and lava rock reminders of destruction,
renewal. All the documentaries, the books,
couldn't prepare me for that.

6

How unfair to get sick from the cold lip
of a water bottle! Or from water itself—
my heart breaks even as life's
spectrum seems so bright to me now—
prismatic and rainbowy, all those
sparkling solstice lights warming December,
me and the grandson having our
lucky lives together. At Arches,
Utah, I photographed 300 million years
of salt and sandstone and shale,
a layer cake of geological history, proving
we will all be squished like bugs one day
and added to the bone pile. Sometimes
I'm okay with that. Today, tooth #21
was yanked from my mouth to Procol Harum.
Then I came home and ate grits with Velveeta,
a word I thought I'd never use in a poem,
but there you go: one more indisputable bone.

7

I'm so sorry to hear about your tooth
gone from your mouth. Our teeth last
even longer than our bones, but where
are pulled teeth scattered? And what
will a future explorer make of one lone tooth
without its partners? I once wore earrings
made from a boyfriend's wisdom
teeth. He wrapped them in a wire loop
and everyone agreed it was gruesome
except him. And me. Death seemed far away
and ironic. We were in college in Boston,
but soon he transferred and I can't remember
why. How can our hearts smash and then,
in the repairing, forget? I love grits.
I love Velveeta. I love baby food desserts
that come in tiny jars. I used to heat Gerber
Blueberry Buckle in a pan of water
for my nieces and, when they'd had enough,
I'd run my finger inside the glass—
it tasted like pie filling, only better.
I have no idea where those earrings are now.

8

And bones, I bet, come in brilliant colors
in other more precocious dimensions. And teeth
glow beneath black light in the back room
of Buddha's & Goudha's smoke shop.
Today is Christmas and our children
are comatose with delight. Last night
a young woman was raped at knifepoint,
her bones rattling in her ears.
Follow your inner moonlight, said Ginsberg,
in touch at once with magic and ache.
A heart holds so much more than we think it can,
or more than we think it should. Now there's
a baby meeting a snowman for the first time
and I long for the kind of justice
a woman needs whose spirit has been snuffed.
Thumpity thump thump, thumpity thump.
I send her to you surrounded by light.
My bones are blue with grief.

9

O, Maureen, sometimes I squelch my happiness—
the thought of rape just around the corner,
then the actual rape. People we love. I hate cop
shows—a man in blue determined
to find the young girl's murderer.
(Why are the dead on TV so young
and beautiful?) And at the end
of an hour justice is served, except
the girl is still dead. And every woman watching
is reminded again how the world is ready
to treat her. So I send a sword of light,
which is nothing like the light from a screen.
I send light that makes a protective shield
around that young woman's magenta aura.
Remember when you stopped my asthma attack
with your warm palms? We were in a cab.
I was choking, and you put your hands on my
back and I stopped? I once saw pink
rising like heat from your fingers. In the Amazon
I saw a shrunken head, and as a guide explained
the technique—the boiling, the taking of the skin
from the skull in one piece—I took flight
with a red-bellied macaw.

10

To actually leave our bodies is no easy trick,
yet we excel at it—like soldiers in combat.
I saw no foreshadowing of violence
in our poem, did you? Maybe dogma. Maybe teeth
in a trash bin. It's winter, so what? This rape
occurred in the South where oaks hold their leaves
and bow to each other across centuries.
When your breath eased on that ride through Manhattan,
I was so deep inside my body I could hear
my blood and yours—the cab a hallowed space.
Maybe evolution does violence to our molecules,
reordering, replicating, coercing us to morph.
Now I've got my opposable thumbs, I'm
upright as a bass, I know how to wear underwear
made of silk to protect my bones in snow.
What to do with our outrageous capabilities?
I've wanted to tell you how, here in Colorado,
winter geese are everywhere, ribboning the entire
sky and honking with purpose, if not joy.

§

Questionnaired

after David Ives

Thank you for your very kind letter about our collaborative work. Here are the answers to your questions.

1. Longhand, shorthand, peacock blue, Exquisite Corpse, origami, bank receipt scribbles, Scrabble tiles shaken from the purple velvet bag, computer while eating candied orange slices.
2. After breakfast, during brunch, around many tables, eating, not eating. Cartwheeling on beach (metaphorically, of course, as one of us has sore carpal tunnel wrists). In New York loft sublets, cyberspace, outer space, at Panera until the wifi runs out. Pre wifi we used phones. Pre cell phones we used phone booths, Superwoman style. *Oyl* was written in Queens in a room that no longer exists.
3. Yes.
4. No.
5. Of course!
6. Uncle Will and Uncle Leo.
7. It was 1990. Our first poem, "Ecofeminism in the Year 2000," was very serious. We didn't really know what ecofeminism was but it sounded serious and we were serious back then and we wanted to do something serious. But we included a joke in the poem, which had to do with one of our spouses, and she has never forgiven us for that.
8. David Trinidad and Bob Flanagan.

9. Ice cream sandwiches.
10. Surrealists.
11. No, we never have. Too messy.
12. D: When I was ten, I wrote lyrics to a series of country songs I twanged in my head. I never liked country music, though my father adored Tex Ritter's "Blood in the Saddle." I wrote the lyrics because I saw an ad that producers were looking for lyrics and would pay "big money." These were my first forays into poems. M: It was May in the seventh grade. The nuns ran a poetry contest for the best poem about Mary (the Mother of God, etc.), and I won. It had stanzas—maybe tercets. I remember it was very blue.
13. We've taken naps in the same bed. Does that count? Just kidding. We are two femmes, silly! Both of us, for better or worse, are attracted to "male" energy. Not that it's any of your business.
14. When we signed a book for someone who had bought it used and crossed out the original dedication, "To Mary Jo."
15. Pajamas.
16. We left our collaborative relationship for two years once and the only ones who noticed were Kristine and Jay.
17. When the Miami Book Fair gave us the Sunday 10 a.m. reading slot. Or maybe it was the time the neo-formalists called us witches.
18. When we saw our Olive Oyl poems brought to life in a theater piece by Emily Rems. She directed men and women who wore black bun wigs and red skirts. How exciting to see our words come out of other people's mouths as though our poems were part of a breathing pop-up book! Maureen was overheard muttering, "I'm so overwhelmed" and weeping happily. Denise thought, "Wait a minute. Why aren't we more famous?"
19. Yes.
20. Yes.

21. Muriel Rukeyser. Who else?
22. *Caprice* is the title of our latest book and it's with Sibling Rivalry Press. Some of our friends asked us what the word caprice means. Others wondered if it meant we were changing our sexual orientations. No, we said, although one of us said later: Maybe. Basically, we said, *Caprice* is just *Caprice.*
23. Miss Scarlet did it with Mrs. Peacock in the conservatory.
24. The anhinga.
25. Did you mean "poem" or "porn"? Actually, for us, there's not a big difference.
26. "Litany of the Fathers" would be a good example of a poem about patriarchy gone awry, after we read it to a real audience, even after we gave everyone an indulgence of seven years and/or a plenary indulgence once a month if recited daily. Not sure why so many people got pissed off. Ingrates.
27. We wrote "A Crown of Spells to Ward off Susans" to release us from the fears we had about two women who were threatening our romantic relationships with our partners at the time. They both had the same name—and neither was a Susan. A Susan one of us knew wrote a few years later to say, next time you want to say something about me, say it to my face.
28. We're not witches ourselves, obviously, or we'd have a lot more money, be really thin, and never age, but in a lot of our poems we pretended to know a witch or two. "Crashing Witch" is about the witch you see riding her broomstick into doors. Recently, women are taking witches off broomsticks which they say are phallic and setting them in convertibles which are still pretty phallic, but at least it would hurt a lot less as the witch crashes into a tree.
29. Pajamas.
30. "But the true feminist deals out of a lesbian consciousness whether or not she ever sleeps with women." (Audre Lorde)

§

Acknowledgments

Sincere thanks to the editors of the following publications in which some of the poems in this collection first appeared:

The American Journal of Poetry—"Anti(dis)establishmentarianism Sonnet"

Best American Poetry Blog, March 31, 2020—"Equinox"

PoetsArtists—"Number's Up," "Pomp & Pyrotechnics"

Green Mountains Review—"This Different Life," as "10 Days in March (This Different Life)"

Indiana Review—"Questionnaired"

LiveMag!—"'A is for Alpha' & Other Axed Sesame Street Songs"

MiPOesias—"If Not Joy" (Nin Andrews, guest editor)

Ocean State Review—"What We Write about When We Don't Write about the Pandemic"

Pleiades—"Credo," 12 Lines about Gender (Retro)," "Solstice"

Plume—"Floridada: Our 51st State," "Songs of Hierarchy & Hoodie"

Poem-a-Day, Academy of American Poets—"Florida Doll Sonnet"

Posit—"12 Lines about Gender (Florida-style)," "12 Lines about Gender (the Cosmos)"

Prairie Schooner—"Holy Hippocampus," "Heroic"

Rattle—"Stairway to Heaven Sonnet"

South Florida Poetry Journal (*SoFloPoJo*)—"Howl," "Resurrection Sonnets," "14 Lines about Water," "27 Lines about Death"

Under a Warm Green Linden—"Death Is Not a Riddle," "Yes, And," "13 Lines about Walls"

*

"Florida Doll Sonnet" also appeared in *The Doll Collection*, Terrapin Books, Diane Lockward, ed. 2016.

"Stairway to Heaven Sonnet" was reprinted in Extra Virgin Press's *Home* Broadside Series for the Miami Book Fair, 2017 (Tom Virgin, printmaker, Michelle Weinberg, visual artist).

"12 Lines about Gender (Retro)" also appeared on *Verse Daily*, July 10, 2024.

Tom Virgin (Extra Virgin Press, Miami), letterpress and fine artist, designed and printed a limited edition of *Q42P* (*Questionnaire for Two Pussies*) as an artist's chapbook featuring the poems "Pomp & Pyrotechnics," "Holy Hippocampus: A Conversation in Couplets," "Florida Doll Sonnet," "Anti(dis)establishmentarianism Sonnet," "If Not Joy," and "Questionnaired," along with artist Mary Malm.

About the Authors

MAUREEN SEATON (1947-2023) authored twenty-three poetry collections, both solo and collaborative—most recently *The Sky Is an Elephant* (ELJ Editions, 2023); *Undersea* (Jackleg Press, 2021); and *Sweet World* (CavanKerry Press, 2019), winner of the Florida Book Award in Poetry. Her honors include Lambda Literary Awards for both lesbian memoir and lesbian poetry, the Audre Lorde Award, an NEA fellowship, and the Pushcart Prize. She was professor emerita of creative writing at the University of Miami and was voted Miami's Best Poet 2020 by the readers of the *Miami New Times*.

DENISE DUHAMEL is, most recently, the author of *Pink Lady* (Pitt Poetry Series, 2025), *Second Story* (Pittsburgh, 2021) and *Scald* (Pittsburgh, 2017). *Blowout* (Pittsburgh, 2013) was a finalist for the National Book Critics Circle Award. *In Which* (2024) is a winner of the Rattle Chapbook Prize. Her other titles include *Ka-Ching!*; *Two and Two*; *Queen for a Day: Selected and New Poems*; *The Star-Spangled Banner*; and *Kinky*. Her nonfiction has appeared in *The New York Times* and her book of lyric essays with Julie Marie Wade is *The Unrhymables: Collaborations in Prose* (Noctuary Press, 2019). A recipient of NEA and Guggenheim Fellowships, she is a distinguished university professor at Florida International University in Miami.